Stories in Welsh Stone

THE SECRETS WITHIN 15 WELSH GRAVES

Stories in Welsh Stone

The secrets within 15 Welsh graves

Geoff Brookes

Published in 2008 by
Welsh Country magazine
Aberbanc, Llandysul, Ceredigion SA44 5NP
www.welshcountry.co.uk
Tel: 01559 372010

ISBN 978-0-95587350-8

A CIP record for this title is available from the British Library

Some of the text in this book has previously been published in
Welsh Country magazine.

Please note : Great care has been taken to ensure that the information
contained in this book is accurate. However as many of the subjects were not
of great notoriety and now cannot answer for themselves, neither the author
nor the publisher can accept legal responsibility or liability for any loss or
damage caused by reliance upon the accuracy of the information herein.

Designed and edited by Welsh Country Design

Printed by Gomer Press, Ceredigion

To Liz, without whom I would be lost

CONTENTS

PREFACE

The starting point has always been a gravestone. Odd really, when you consider that a gravestone represents an ending. It is a full stop at the end of a life. It is where all our stories will end.

It may seem a curious pastime, seeking out the stories that lie behind the stones. But for me, more than anything else, these memorials bring the past alive. They are not stories only about death; they are more about life.

Some people have lives that are exceptional. Others become interesting in the manner of their death. But everyone, surely, has a story to tell and it is our duty to listen.

All of the people in this book were people just like you and me: the same emotions, the same aspirations, the same inadequacies. They merely wore different clothes.

We need to remember our past, for it is the past that has made us what we are today. As you read these stories you can see that what motivates people has never changed very much. We are still the same as we have always been. It is just that today we have more buttons to press. We all still pursue happiness and contentment and some of us still never find it.

These are not happy tales. In fact there are some awful stories here. Margaret Williams, John Thomas, Mary Morgan, Elizabeth Jones. Ordinary names. Ordinary people. Ordinary lives. All then suddenly and unexpectedly transformed by extra-ordinary events. Their stories need to be remembered. They need to be preserved and I hope I have done something here to make sure that they are not forgotten. You will find inside this book the tales that now live within fifteen nineteenth century gravestones. They come from across Wales and from the whole range of that momentous century. They speak of infanticide, shipwreck, anorexia and murder.

To reconstruct these stories I have read much and the words you read do become part of what you try to create. The books that have helped me I have acknowledged at the end. Other writers have walked along these same paths as me. Perhaps they have stopped to look at different things. But as much as I can I have gone back to contemporary sources.

I should like to thank Kath and Ian at Welsh Country magazine who have made this book happen. Nine of the stories covered here first appeared in the magazine and without their encouragement I would neither have written the new pieces, nor expanded the original ones. They are the ones who took the risk of publishing these stories in the first place.

Lastly and most importantly I must thank my wife Liz who has supported and helped throughout, patiently trailing around the country from obscure church and chapel, to wet overgrown cemetery. I would never have found any of these graves without her - she reads the map. &

Our Journey...

Mary Morgan, Presteigne

Thomas Heslop, Newcastle Emlyn

Elizabeth Jones, Gwynfe

Margaret Williams, Cadoxton

John Price, Llanafan Fawr

Adeline Coquelin, Pembrey

Mary Kavanagh, Penrice

Richard Lewis, Aberafan

Eleanor Williams, Felindre

Jane Lewis, Tonyrefail

Joseph Butler, Llanafan

Sarah Jacob, Llanfihangel ar Arth

John Johnes, Caio

John Thomas, Kidwelly

Arthur Linton, Aberdare

Mary Morgan

HANGED FOR INFANTICIDE

1804

PRESTEIGNE

THIS IS THE MOST DISTURBING OF TALES

You will find her grave in a prominent position in the graveyard of St. Andrew's Church in the centre of Presteigne. Walk down Broad Street past the Judge's Lodging Museum and the church is at the bottom of the road on the left hand side. Go into the church yard and the two gravestones are on your left, the small one - which is an original - facing the large one - which is a copy. The original stone is displayed in The Judge's Lodging.

© Ordnance Survey, Anquet Technology

Whatever the wrong that Mary Morgan did, how could they have hanged her? Just 17 years of age and carried to her death on a cart in Presteigne.

t begins in an all too-familiar way. A young servant, only 16, living away from home. Pregnant. In denial. And then...

If you ever needed to find evidence of the strict divisions brought about by the class system, you can see it here in this case - in the fate handed down to Mary, and in the sanctimonious claptrap carved upon her headstone by her betters. Betters who sought to make her an example but were themselves responsible for very many other pregnant servant girls. Betters - one of whom was, according to some fanciful accounts, himself

13

responsible for Mary's child. For there is indeed a version that would have her legally murdered by the ruling classes to keep their indiscretions a secret.

From the very beginning this is a cruel tale. A heartless crime. A pointless punishment.

In the fascinating Judge's Lodging in Presteigne, you are guided through the restored rooms of a fine and elegant house, just as it was in the nineteenth century. Below these rooms you enter the dank cells, from which you suddenly emerge, blinking,

HOW CLOSE THEY MUST ALL HAVE STOOD TO HER AS THEY HEARD THE SENTENCE OF DEATH

into the dock in the courtroom, just like the one where Mary stood, dressed in jolly clothes, confused, bewildered. How close they must all have stood to her. You wonder how deeply they will have looked into her eyes as they heard the sentence of death. They could not have distanced themselves from her in such a small space. A child herself, suddenly facing unrelenting judicial revenge.

Of course it was an awful crime. But it was an awful punishment.

The story begins in Maesllwch Castle, near Glasbury, just outside Hay on Wye. It was the home of Walter Wilkins, Member of Parliament, who employed Mary as under-cook. She was 16 years old and came from Llowes, the daughter of Elizabeth and Rees Morgan.

On Sunday 23 September 1804 she appeared to be unwell and was sent back to the room she shared with the under-dairymaid, who was away visiting her sister. It was here that she gave birth to a baby girl. A frightened child giving birth to an unwanted child, Mary killed it, almost severing the head with a penknife. She slashed open the mattress and stuffed the little body inside. Then she hid the knife under a pillow. Such woeful attempts at concealment should really have alerted someone to her state of mind. But that is not how things happened. Her crime was almost instantly discovered by the other servants who had suspected for some time that she was pregnant. It was an open and shut case.

The inquest on the baby was held in Glasbury two days later before the Coroner, Hector Cooksey, who was the landlord of the Radnorshire Arms in Presteigne. It wasn't hard to establish the facts.

St. Andrew's Church in Presteigne

OF COURSE IT WAS AN AWFUL CRIME.
BUT IT WAS AN AWFUL PUNISHMENT

'Mary Morgan, a single woman, on the 23 day of September being big with child, afterwards alone and secretly from her body did bring forth alive a female child, which by the laws and customs of this kingdom was a bastard. Mary Morgan, moved and seduced by the instigation of the devil afterwards on the same day feloniously, wilfully and of her malice aforethought did make an assault with a certain penknife and gave the child one mortal wound. The child instantly died.'

What else could be said?

Mary was too ill to travel to the County Gaol in Presteigne immediately, but was moved in early October. She was imprisoned for six months, awaiting her trial for infanticide. In April 1805, just after her seventeenth birthday, she appeared before Justice Hardinge.

It would appear that up until the very final moments, Mary believed that he would treat her leniently. It was highly unusual for the death sentence to be carried out in such cases of infanticide. It was not regarded in the same way as murder; it was seen more as a complication of pregnancy. Even in those days there was a vague awareness of post-natal depression. Normal practice was for a death sentence to be immediately reprieved. Indeed, Hardinge had done such a thing only a week before in Brecon.

However, Mary appears to have upset him through her attitude and behaviour. She did not seem to understand the seriousness of her situation. Hardinge wrote that:

> 'she took it for granted that she would be acquitted, had ordered gay apparel, to attest the event of her deliverance and supposed the young gentleman (whom I knew well) would save her by a letter to me.'

IT WOULD APPEAR THAT UP UNTIL THE VERY FINAL MOMENTS, MARY BELIEVED THAT SHE WOULD BE TREATED LENIENTLY

Now what is this? A 'young gentleman'? Well, it is a detail that has helped many to construct an elaborate and appealing conspiracy theory around these awful circumstances. For the "young gentleman" in question was Walter Wilkins Junior, her boss' son. Who was also a member of the jury.

SHE WAS
CONDEMNED TO
DEATH AND HE
DIRECTED THAT
HER BODY SHOULD
BE DELIVERED TO
THE SURGEONS, TO
BE 'DISSECTED AND
ANATOMISED'

To the Memory of Mary Morgan,
who young and beautiful, endowed
with a good understanding and
disposition, but unenlightened by the
sacred truths of Christianity became
the victim of sin and shame and
was condemned to an ignominious
death on the 11th April 1805,
for the Murder of her bastard Child

Rous'd to a first sense of guilt and
remorse by the eloquent and humane
exertions of her benevolent Judge,
Mr. Justice Hardinge, she underwent
the Sentence of the Law on the
following Thursday with unfeigned
repentance and a furvent hope of
forgivenefs through the merits of a
redeeming intercefsor.
This Stone is erected not merely to
perpetuate the remembrance of a
departed penitent but to remind the
living of the frailty of humannature
when unsupported by Religion

Thomas Bruce Brudenell Bruce Earl of
AILESBURY

Freespirit Images

THE RESIDENTS DREW THEIR CURTAINS ON THE
MORNING OF HER EXECUTION AND NO FARMER WAS
PREPARED TO LEND A CART TO TAKE HER TO HER DEATH

Thus the argument goes that he was the father of the child and that he had indeed encouraged her to commit murder, even lending her the penknife that she could not herself afford, to carry out the dreadful crime. The Judge, a friend of the family, did his best to protect young Walter and preserve his imminent engagement to a well-heeled Hereford girl. The ruling classes, looking after their own. It cost them little, other than the life of a servant girl. Still, plenty more where she came from.

If that story doesn't suit you, then why not believe that the Judge himself had fathered the child on a visit to Maesllwch. He was, after all, a friend of the family. That is why Mary expected deliverance. That is why she behaved as she did. This was no judge, this was her lover. Thus Mary once again becomes victim of an establishment cover up.

It is all highly unlikely. A fellow servant at the castle believed he was the father, though paternity could never be anything other than an opinion. It is maternity that is the fact. So the known facts were that Mary was both the mother and the killer. She did it. That was never in question.

She was found guilty. Hardinge was convinced that there 'was no single trace of religion to be found in her thoughts.' He was horrified by the premeditated nature of the killing, planned even before the onset of labour. As far as he could see, she had denied the very essence of her womanhood. Hardinge was unrelenting and his final address to her was described as consisting of 'pious platitudes, without pity or understanding.'

She was condemned to death and he directed that her body should be delivered to the surgeons, to be 'dissected and anatomised.'

There was no reprieve. Two days later, on Saturday 13 April 1805 she was executed at noon at Gallows Lane, on the west side of Presteigne.

Stories have grown about poor Mary. About how the residents drew their curtains out of respect on the morning of her execution. How they couldn't find a farmer prepared to lend them a cart to take her to her death. How she was carried unconscious in a shroud from the cart to the scaffold, her long tresses flowing. How a gentleman raced to London for a reprieve, but was delayed by his horse going lame and so arrived back too late; how on his subsequent visits to Presteigne, Hardinge laid flowers at her grave, writing verses in her memory. Romantic notions, probably. The sort of stories that people invent when they must confront the horror that has been committed in their name. Hardinge had no time for doubt. He did what he believed was his duty and then moved on.

THERE WAS NO REPRIEVE. ON SATURDAY 13 APRIL, 1805 MARY WAS EXECUTED AT GALLOWS LANE, PRESTEIGNE

It was his friend, Thomas Bruce, the Earl of Aylesbury, who sponsored the gravestone, perhaps to counteract the criticism Hardinge received for his sentence. It is a remarkable piece, unlike anything else you are likely to see. The original is on display in the Judge's Lodging, whilst a replica stands over Mary in the grave yard of St. Andrew's Church.

It is breathtaking in its pomposity:

To the memory of Mary Morgan, who young and beautiful, endowed with a good understanding and disposition, but unenlightened by the sacred truths of Christianity became the victim of sin and shame and was condemned to an ignominious death on the 11th April 1805, for the murder of her bastard child.

Rous'd to a first sense of guilt and remorse by the eloquent and humane exertions of her benevolent Judge, Mr Justice Hardinge, she underwent the Sentence of Law on the following Thursday with unfeigned repentance and a fervent hope of forgiveness through the merits of a redeeming intercessor.

This stone is erected not merely to perpetuate the remembrance of a departed penitent, but to remind the living of the frailty of human nature when unsupported by Religion.

Clearly the judge did her a favour.

Others were outraged by this awful stone. Another grave stone was erected facing those empty words. Who paid for this second stone? Her parents, her defence counsel, the townspeople? No one knows. But it stands there as an act of defiance. It is small and faded, but it speaks of her age, of her suffering and perhaps it speaks for most of us too.

In memory of Mary Morgan who suffer'd April 13th 1805. Aged 17 years. He that is without sin among you Let him first cast a stone at her. The 8th Chapr. Of John, part of ye 7th vr.

Mary Morgan. Only 17 and marked by two gravestones. &

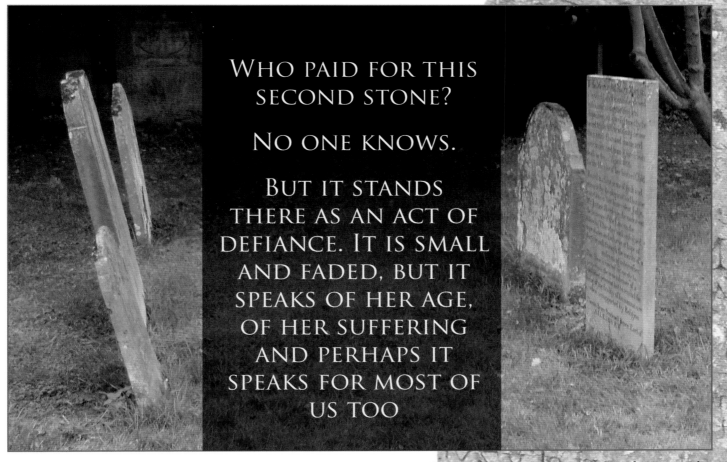

WHO PAID FOR THIS
SECOND STONE?

NO ONE KNOWS.

BUT IT STANDS
THERE AS AN ACT OF
DEFIANCE. IT IS SMALL
AND FADED, BUT IT
SPEAKS OF HER AGE,
OF HER SUFFERING
AND PERHAPS IT
SPEAKS FOR MOST OF
US TOO

Mary Morgan's two gravestones face one another

Thomas Heslop
SHOT

1814

NEWCASTLE EMLYN

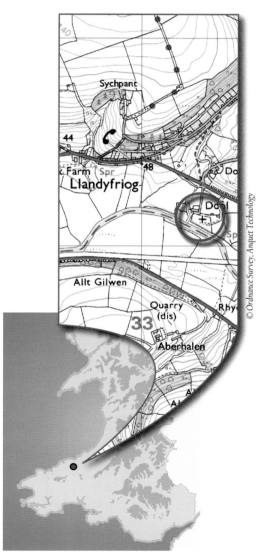

Your destination is St. Tyfriog Church in Llandyfriog, on the banks of the River Teifi. Drive out of Newcastle Emlyn along the A475 towards Lampeter and you will reach Llandyfriog after about a mile. Just past the village, turn down a long drive on the right to the church. There is plenty of space to park.

Heslop's grave is a rectangular tomb. Walk through the churchyard to the rear of the church. The large chest with its faint, but still readable inscription, is close to the wall of the church.

Left: View across the Teifi valley from Llandyfriog

Five men in a field, meeting in accordance with well-established rules. For two of them, their honour and pride had been so ravaged that there could only be one way in which the affront could be resolved.

A duel.

Thomas Heslop and John Beynon were accompanied by their seconds and a local doctor was in attendance, ready to pick up the pieces.

It was Saturday 10 September 1814 and they had all come together in Danwarrin field in Llandyfriog near Adpar, which is just the other side of the river from Newcastle Emlyn.

The field they had selected was divided by a stream. Beynon and Heslop stood on either side of the stream, facing away from each other. The rules were re-stated by their seconds, Walters and Hughes. They were to walk 10 paces before turning and firing.

Neither would, nor could, pull out now. There was no going back.

© Ordnance Survey, Anquet Technology

Abi Thrift

They began to pace out their deliberate steps.

Who can tell what thoughts were flashing through their minds as they counted down towards such an awful conclusion? Just a few short steps separating them from injury or vindication, or possibly both. One, two three, four...

THIS WAS A SHOCKING AFFRONT TO THE ACCEPTED RULES OF ENGAGEMENT

Except that things did not go according to plan. Because after only five paces Beynon turned and shot Heslop in the back. He died almost immediately.

This was a shocking affront to the accepted rules of engagement. But when self preservation is paramount and the adrenaline is pumping furiously, it is an action that we can perhaps understand. He hadn't played by the rules, but who amongst us has been in his position? How many of us today could have calmly measured out those 10 steps, knowing what might be at their conclusion?

John Beynon was a local solicitor who owned a small farm called Llwyncadfor.

He may also have served as coroner for Carmarthen. He enjoyed his status as a landowner and was probably something of a wheeler-dealer. We know for example that he had recently sold land at auction following the death of his mother. Most importantly however, Beynon was a man who enjoyed his shooting. This was how he met Thomas Heslop.

Heslop had been born in Kingston, Jamaica and was currently living in Carmarthen. He was 34. He appears to have been very well connected, as we can see in his last will and testament, written on Friday 9 September, the day before the duel and now lodged in the Public Records Office. In it he refers to his friends in Clapham and to his wife Elizabeth. He appoints his son Abraham in Surrey as an executor. To his second at the duel, 'my esteemed friend John Walters,' he leaves his double barrelled shotgun and his pistols. Those that were never used. He looks forward to meeting them all 'in another, better world.' Was he truly apprehensive? Or was he confident of his ability to blast a hole in an irritating country solicitor?

So what could have happened that brought these men so suddenly to confront the possibility of death in an undistinguished field in West Wales?

Thomas Heslop's grave

BEYNON TURNED AND SHOT HESLOP IN THE BACK. HE DIED ALMOST IMMEDIATELY

St. Tyfriog Church in Llandyfriog

HESLOP CALLED BEYNON A VILLAIN AND A SCOUNDREL AND CHALLENGED HIM TO A DUEL. HOW SUDDENLY AND UNEXPECTEDLY IT CAME ABOUT

Heslop was down in Newcastle Emlyn with some of his friends on a shooting party, probably hosted by John Beynon. It hadn't gone well, but they all gathered together at Beynon's invitation for dinner on Thursday 8 September 1814 in the Old Salutation Inn in Adpar.

As the evening wore on a dispute developed. Heslop was not happy because he claimed that he hadn't been permitted to shoot when and where he pleased. He hadn't been able to decimate the partridge population as much as he would have liked. There had been too many restrictions and this had prevented him from having a good time. He put the blame fairly and squarely on Beynon. As host, Beynon tried to take the heat out of the situation by changing the subject. He started to make derogatory remarks about the barmaid, in the manner of pub bores everywhere, questioning her virtue, suggesting her availability.

It is interesting isn't it, that however much times change, the behaviour of drunks in the bar remains the same. This particular laddish moment however, was one that went spectacularly wrong.

Heslop would not be calmed. He had worked up a fine head of steam and now had something more concrete and immediate upon which to focus his anger. He made strong objections to what Beynon said and, in defence of the poor barmaid, slandered by a pompous drunk, called Beynon a villain and a scoundrel and challenged him to a duel. Beynon accepted.

How suddenly and unexpectedly it came about. Heslop must have been confident of his ability to win, or he would not have pursued so trivial a circumstance. His confidence was such that it obviously unsettled Beynon. His local reputation demanded that he should respond, but he

THE LOCAL PEOPLE WERE OUTRAGED AT SUCH DISHONOURABLE CONDUCT; IT WAS A SHOCKING THING TO HAVE DONE

probably found himself out of his depth, in the horrifying position of facing death at the hands of a skilled gunman as a result of an ill-judged and boozy comment about a barmaid. If he could only turn back time.......

Perhaps this is the reason he shot Heslop in the back. But whatever the reason, the local people were outraged at such dishonourable conduct. It was a shocking thing to have done. But then it all got worse.

BEYNON WAS TO REMAIN IN PRISON ONLY UNTIL HIS FINE WAS PAID.
HE WAS FINED ONE SHILLING

At his trial in Cardigan, Beynon was found guilty of manslaughter, which was probably the only verdict the jury could have returned. However, consider the fact that in the court records his legal status is confirmed; Beynon is described as an attorney. It is easy to believe that his colleagues arranged events for him as he escaped any sort of lengthy prison term; he was to remain in prison only until his fine was paid.

And he was fined one shilling.

Public opinion was outraged at this perceived injustice. Did the people of Cardiganshire object to the way he had transgressed against the accepted code of the gentleman, or was it that they just didn't like him? Whichever it was, they were after him. It is said that he had to go into hiding in a cellar near the bridge in Newcastle Emlyn to escape summary justice. He fled to America, so they say. Whilst the man from the West Indies stayed behind in a small country churchyard in West Wales.

Abi Thrift

Left: the bridge at Newcastle Emlyn

Of course the past is never still. It is always ripe for re-interpretation. There are those who would now exonerate Beynon, who say that the traditional tale is wrong; that he didn't shoot Heslop in the back. But whatever new research might reveal, he still lies in a Welsh cemetery.

Heslop's grave has subsided slightly along one side and although the slab that faces the rain has worn, you can still determine what it says:

Sacred
To the Memory of
Thomas Heslop.
Born 27 June 1780
Died 10 September 1814.
Alas Poor Heslop.

Alas indeed. How unexpectedly life can turn out. From Jamaica to a quiet grave by the River Teifi. From Jamaica to become a little footnote in history as the last man to die in a duel in Wales.

Based upon an article that first appeared in Welsh Country magazine in Nov/Dec 2006

Elizabeth Jones
POISONED

1816
GWYNFE

We never thought that we'd find it so easily. After all, it happened such a long time ago

Take the A40 from Llandeilo in Carmarthenshire towards Llandovery. After about five miles you will find a roundabout. Turn right here on the A4069 to Llangadog. Continue along the main road and when you arrive in the centre of the village bear right towards Pontarllechau and Brynamman.

At Pont Newydd turn right and follow the signs to Capel Gwynfe. When you arrive in the village drive through it until you see All Saints Church on the right. You can park easily alongside.

Enter the churchyard through the main gate and you will find Elizabeth's gravestone standing against the right hand side of the old church about 15 yards from the entrance.

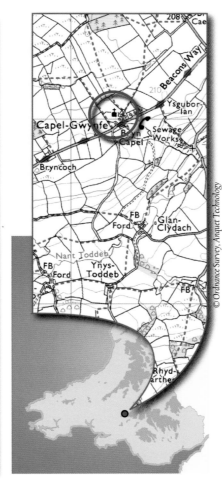

© Ordnance Survey, Anquet Technology

Almost two hundred years ago. But there it was, standing against the wall of the old church. 1816. Elizabeth Jones. 20 years old it says.

The stone is splitting now and the inscription flaking off. A few more years and we will have lost it completely and if those words do disappear, falling off in a jigsaw of flakes into the grass, then we would have an even greater responsibility to remember the awful story that Elizabeth's grave represents. Because hers is a dreadful story, and whatever others may have said, there was only one victim and that was poor Elizabeth Jones.

Her misfortune (and her murderer?) was Rees Thomas Rees.

She lived in Ynys Toddeb farm near Llangadog, Carmarthenshire. Although it is only a few miles from Llandeilo it was quite an isolated place, and perhaps that sense of distance or isolation brings a certain intensity to relationships. This was certainly how her tragedy began. She was courted by a young man called Rees Thomas Rees who was a few years older than her. He was 26 and was described as an honest and honourable man who occasionally preached for the Presbyterian chapel in Llangadog. It appears that they intended to marry, but Elizabeth's parents, Llywelyn and Luzzod, weren't too keen. At 19 years of age they felt she was too young. If they had any other reservations about the young gentleman, they are not recorded. Parental consent was crucial of course, but it cannot, alone, entirely control those fundamental human drives that can wash over all of us. Consent or otherwise made little difference.

It is probable that they developed their relationship through the old Welsh custom of bundling. The couple would lie side by side in bed, talking. It was called 'car war y gwely' - courting in bed - and as you might imagine, bundling was blamed for all kinds of immorality, not to mention high levels of rural illegitimacy. Elizabeth was just another young girl caught out by tradition, because soon she was pregnant. It was early May 1816. Here was a dilemma that the two of them had to face and which they tried to resolve as many had done before them. Marriage was forbidden and Elizabeth particularly

had to face public shame and condemnation. They decided to terminate the pregnancy. We cannot be sure to what extent this was a mutual decision; we do not know what emotional pressure was exerted by either party. What Rees claimed later was that Elizabeth asked him to buy the medication to do the necessary. This was impossible to verify, but given other evidence that emerged, it sounds as if it was quite probable.

This is what he did. He went to the May Fair in Llandeilo and obtained supplies from Joseph Yeomans, surgeon. We can't be sure what he got, but the charge that Rees faced mentions mercury, arsenic and savin. She needed it apparently 'for purging her blood.' At least this is what he claimed. Everyone would have known what this particular euphemism stood for. In doing this Rees was connecting himself to an age-old tradition. Methods of inducing abortion have been around forever. Five thousand years ago the Chinese Emperor Shennong prescribed mercury to his overworked concubines. The Greeks and the Romans believed in dosing pregnant women with near-fatal levels of poison. These poisons were not necessarily taken orally either. It was a brutal unpleasant business, but people knew what to do and usually knew who to consult. Women quite naturally passed the knowledge between themselves. The herbal remedies were well

Freespirit Images

THE CHARGE THAT REES FACED MENTIONS MERCURY,
ARSENIC AND SAVIN. SHE NEEDED IT, APPARENTLY,
'FOR PURGING HER BLOOD'

Elizabeth seems to have taken a rich combination of herbal remedies before Rees turned up with the nuclear option

known. Hemp, called 'The Devil's Flower', was employed. Another popular application was the root of a type of fern, which was called in French 'Prostitute Root.' Savin was also frequently employed. It is a type of juniper and this is one of the substances that Rees was accused of administering. Elizabeth seems to have already taken a rich combination of these herbal remedies before he turned up with the nuclear option. To be fair to him, it might well have been her reaction to a combination of those country solutions that induced such an extreme toxic reaction. But in the absence of any other evidence, the court at the time felt that the arsenic was perhaps a step too far.

Rees gave the medication to Elizabeth and she almost immediately became ill. Significantly he called a doctor, though not Nathaniel Rees who usually attended the family. Instead he called upon Joseph Yeomans who had sold him the stuff. Quite how he managed to do this without alerting her parents is unclear, but it is plainly stated in Rees' arraignment and it is an important

detail in understanding Rees' subsequent conviction. Whatever Yeomans did, had little effect. Perhaps he said that it was only to be expected in the circumstances and to sit out what was obviously merely minor discomfort. "Don't worry," he might have said, "this is perfectly normal..." Anyway, when this house-call was complete Rees, having ensured that a generous dose had been taken, apparently went off home.

After midnight her sister Gwenllian was awakened by the sound of Elizabeth's groans. She found her rolling around on the floor in agony. The poor girl was in a shocking state. Her body was swollen and blood was oozing from her mouth. She told Gwenllian what had happened very clearly, in what was to become a crucial part of the trial. Rees had given her a grey liquid. She had immediately become ill, but Rees had insisted that she take three doses. It burnt her throat, which soon became ulcerated; her gums and cheeks were swollen to the extent that her whole mouth seized up. Her teeth became black and so loose that she was able to pull them out and give them to her mother. She died a few hours later, having miscarried, on 26 May 1816.

The Cambrian Newspaper a week later names Rees as a murderer. It was not a label from which he could escape. There were people who were very keen to talk to him. The paper also reports that the magistrates decided:

> 'to request all apothecaries, druggists, and chymists to be particular in registering the name and residence of all persons who apply for, or purchase, any poison or noxious drug.'

This, they hope, will:

> 'prevent the general and nefarious use of so pernicious and fatal an article.'

Fat chance.

Such poisonings were not unusual. In fact in some areas, desperate women would consult shepherds and use remedies more commonly prescribed to sheep, without any clear understanding of how it might affect them.

Thomas Hardy's notorious poem 'A Sunday Morning Tragedy' deals with just such a death resulting from abortion medication. It is called 'physic for untimely fruit' and a mother obtains it for her daughter from a shepherd. But it all goes horribly wrong.

> 'Mother, instead of rescue nigh,
> She faintly breathed, alas for me,
> I feel as I were like to die,
> And underground soon, soon
> should be.'

IT HAD NEVER BEEN HIS INTENTION TO KILL HER. HE WAS ONLY TRYING TO SAVE HER FROM THE SHAME OF AN ILLEGITIMATE CHILD

What makes Hardy's poem a tragedy is that the lover changes his mind and returns home, agreeing finally to marry the unfortunate girl, though too late. In our story, Rees Rees never went home at all. He ran away. It is pretty clear that he knew something was up and he wasn't going to stick around to explore the details. By September, Rees 'who is still at large' was committed to trial:

> 'for having administered poison to Elizabeth Jones with a view of producing abortion, but which caused her death.'

It is said that he had decided that he would go to America to start a new life, which is pretty rich when you consider the state in which he had left his beloved. He got as far as Liverpool before changing his mind. He decided to return to Carmarthenshire and hand himself in, convinced that no one could possibly question his motives. He was entirely innocent of any intention to commit murder. His friends, who tried to persuade him otherwise, were simply misguided.

This was a fatal miscalculation.

He was arrested on his return and tried for murder. His defence was that Elizabeth had taken numerous mixtures in the days leading up to her death. Many of these had been provided for her by relatives. How could anyone say that one particular drug was responsible when another was not? It had never been his intention to kill her. He was only trying to save her from the shame of an illegitimate child. The fact that the child was his own does not seem to have impacted upon his argument.

However he had not bargained for Gwenllian. Her evidence about what had happened was vital. It was considered to be a dying declaration by Elizabeth, who had pointed the finger directly at the potion Rees had given her. If she had said it, it must be true. Testimonies to the previous good character of the accused cut no ice. His behaviour in obtaining the medication,

his preference for Yeomans, his flight to Liverpool were sufficient. The jury returned and found him guilty. He was sentenced to execution on Saturday 19 April 1817.

His execution was quite an event, rather like some sort of revivalist meeting. It is said that at least 10,000 people turned up at Babell Hill in Pensarn, just outside Carmarthen, to watch. You can't help thinking that there might have been a certain additional frisson in watching the execution of a preacher man. An opportunity to watch the unmasking of hypocrisy. Of course Rees was no better than the rest of us. Driven by the same desires, consumed by the same fears. Imperfect. Vulnerable. Flawed. But most of the rest of us didn't preach otherwise............

Ministers started praying; the crowd joined in. Rees joined in. There was an orgy of hymn singing. This went on for over an hour. Then Rees addressed the crowd and recited a prayer.

> "Thou didst save the thief on the cross. Oh cleanse thou me! Cleanse me. Cleanse me from my sins. I am found wanting in the balance in this world."

Then, as the executioner kicked away the steps on which he was standing, Rees cried out,

Freespirit Images

Gwenllian's evidence about what had happened was vital; it was considered to be a dying declaration by Elizabeth

"Now I am trembling on the borders of eternity - Farewell."

As the court had instructed, his body was dissected before burial. But the story doesn't end there. In his death Rees Thomas Rees became a warning to others.

She had her life stolen from her in the most dreadful of circumstances

'It is a very wicked habit for young men and women to be courting at untimely hours. In those places where this wicked custom prevails, fornication and uncleanliness overspreads the country...an hour or two before bedtime would be sufficient for young men and women to converse with each other.'

He featured regularly in sermons and in published exhortations concerning the 'many ways that sin has to draw young people astray'. You suspect he would have rather enjoyed this.

'One may be a member of a church and be in a great esteem and yet fall into shameful sins. What has happened to this young man calls loudly on those who stand to take heed lest they fall...The fault was not on religion that he fell into this ditch. Remember Rees Rees.'

But in all of this Elizabeth seems to have been forgotten. It is all about the devil trapping a godly man by exploiting human frailty. Be ever vigilant, because even a preacher can be snatched.

Yes. yes, yes. But what about Elizabeth?

She wasn't just a vessel for his love. She wasn't just the private ear for his sanctimonious claptrap. She was a young girl who had her life stolen from her in the most dreadful of circumstances. She deserves more than to be merely a footnote in the story of a respected man brought down by a moment of weakness.

The poor girl is not difficult to find and Gwynfe is a lovely place to visit anyway. There is just the one road through the village and you will find All Saints in the middle. Elizabeth is there, with her mother Luzzod and her father Llewellyn.

How much they would have wished it otherwise. ◑

Margaret Williams

MURDERED

1823
To record
MURDER
This stone was erected
Over the body
Of
MARGARET WILLIAMS
Aged 26
A native of Carmarthenshire
Living in service in this parish
Who was found dead
With marks of violence upon her person
In a ditch on the marsh
Below this churchyard on the morning
Of Sunday the 14th of July
1822.
Although
The Savage Murderer
Escape for a season the detection of man
Yet God hath set His mark upon him
Either for time or eternity
And
The Cry of Blood
Will assuredly pursue him
To certain and terrible but righteous
JUDGMENT

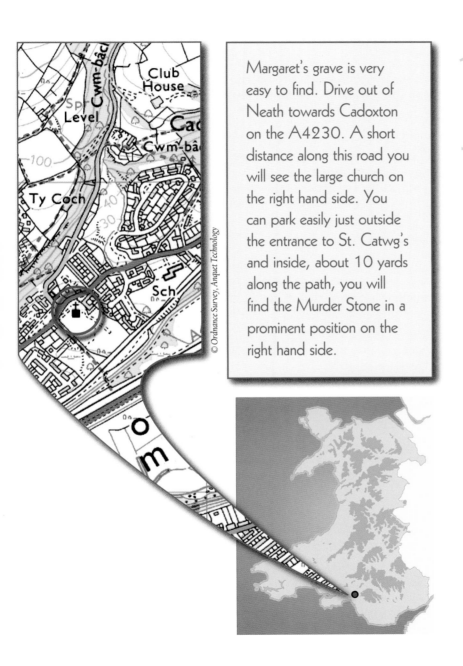

Margaret's grave is very easy to find. Drive out of Neath towards Cadoxton on the A4230. A short distance along this road you will see the large church on the right hand side. You can park easily just outside the entrance to St. Catwg's and inside, about 10 yards along the path, you will find the Murder Stone in a prominent position on the right hand side.

1822

CADOXTON JUXTA NEATH

It is a fine example of a village churchyard. There is a twisted old yew, family vaults, gravestones over two hundred years old. But just inside the gate, there is a Murder Stone.

It stands out because it is not square to the path. It is at an angle to the others around, positioned to face where the murderer lived, but it also stands out because of the words it displays. It speaks of 'murder', 'violence', 'savage,' 'outcry', 'blood' and 'judgement'. The words on the stone are the words of Elijah Waring, a local Quaker and well-known orator, who commissioned the stone to express the outrage of the community at the murder of Margaret Williams and their belief in retribution from which there could never be any escape. The Murderer is truly a man without hope or salvation, for 'God hath set His mark upon him.'

It is in such words that the story unfolds, revealing emotions and dilemmas that join our world with theirs. Of course times change, but people don't. Margaret is merely an ordinary woman wrestling with a familiar crisis, because Margaret was pregnant. What makes her different is that in death she has become a curious footnote in history. Her family, ordinary people with no sense of destiny, were summoned to witness the "heart-rending and appalling spectacle of their murdered child."

The stone stretches out an accusing finger with absolute conviction, silently pointing, undeniable, inflexible, and immovable. It is there on the main path through the village for all to see. The house at which it is aimed has long since gone, replaced by the uniformity of a modern housing estate, but this permanent accusation remains. An act of revenge for an act of brutality.

The story the stone tells can be pieced together from the report that appeared in The Cambrian newspaper a week later, on 20 July 1822. Justice in those days moved with remarkable speed. She was found dead on Sunday morning, 14 July 1822. By Tuesday an inquest was held and an arrest was made. We are told that the jury:

> 'were locked up the whole of
> Tuesday night, an adjournment of
> the inquest being necessary.'

All that was missing was evidence and this was the key point. They couldn't find any evidence.

Margaret was an unmarried country girl from Carmarthenshire. She came from Llangyndeyrn in the Gwendraeth Valley, near Kidwelly. Her father, John Williams, is described as a labourer. She is described as 'a fine, healthy young woman', known for her 'industry and cheerfulness'.

However she was pregnant, probably by at least 16 weeks, and Margaret was adamant about the father of her child. She had announced it publicly on a number of occasions. It was the son of the farmer for whom she worked as a servant. Llewelyn Richard or Richards.

Llewelyn was the one who was arrested for her murder on Tuesday 16 July 1822. The report says clearly that he was 'the man generally suspected of having committed the diabolical act.' But suspicions alone have never been enough. The problem was that there was no proof. All Llewelyn had to do was to keep quiet. There was nothing to link him to the murder. There was nothing to prove that Llewelyn was the father of her child. Paternity, after all, was deniable. Only in recent years has it ever been anything other than a matter of opinion. He could present Margaret as a fantasist, as a country

Freespirit Images

River Neath, Vale of Neath

THE MURDERER IS TRULY A MAN WITHOUT HOPE OR SALVATION, FOR 'GOD HATH SET HIS MARK UPON HIM'

girl on the make. Margaret was older than Llewelyn. She had obviously seduced a younger boy. It probably wasn't his child anyway. You can imagine the scene. She could have proved nothing. The scenes in the farmhouse when she revealed the happy news of her Easter egg can be imagined. Certainly ten weeks previously in May she had moved out - or been thrown out - and was now working for 'an industrious old man who occupies a small cot near Neath'.

ALL LLEWELYN HAD TO DO WAS TO KEEP QUIET; THERE WAS NOTHING TO LINK HIM TO THE MURDER

She had been to Neath on Saturday night. It had been a fine summer's day, though there had been a strong wind. Steam vessels on their way to Ireland, The Saint Patrick and The Duke of Lancaster, had taken shelter in Milford Harbour. Margaret had gone to buy a sheep's head, which was found in her basket along with her hat, on the marsh a short way from her body. She was on her way home. Was it a chance encounter? Was he waiting for her?

Left: St. Catwg's Church, Cadoxton

The report describes her condition:

'... found lying on her left side in a pill on the salt marsh, containing about 30 inches in depth of water...the face and head were under the water, whilst the right side of the body, with the arm in an elevated position, was perfectly dry...the marks on her body consisted of bruises and discolouration on the throat and neck and on both arms above the elbow: but of the two arms the right was most bruised, apparently by strong pressure. Those on the throat were manifestly caused by strangulation.'

So he grabbed her, shook her, strangled her, left her in a ditch and yes, she was pregnant, for they 'opened and examined the body.'

Llewelyn would say nothing. Why should he? What incentive was there to confession? The newspaper always carried reports of recent executions. No, he would keep quiet. So he did. But everyone knew. Or thought they knew. We are told that 'the strongest suspicions existed against the prisoner' but that 'no evidence was adduced to establish his guilt.' There was nothing to link him to her death. The absence of clues was merely an example of 'Human wickedness and cunning.' The verdict therefore was 'Wilful Murder against some person or persons unknown.'

But they knew and their anger and their certainty point like a finger across the centuries.

> 'The magistrates have declared their resolution to seek out fresh evidence with unremitting scrutiny and it is devoutly to be wished that the inhuman monster who perpetrated this foul and horrid deed may yet be brought to justice.'

It is not a person they seek, merely evidence. In language that pre-figures the words of Elijah Waring the report concludes: 'The eye of Providence is upon him.'

Llewelyn may have escaped conviction and execution, but what now could he do? His position within his community was untenable. His family will have known this too.

He fled to Hereford, whilst a donation was sought to build the accusatory headstone. It took a year to have it prepared and erected.

There is a report in the paper on 3 May 1823 about the stone which had been erected three weeks before and was already a local attraction:

> 'Though no directly criminatory evidence was elicited in the course of several judicial enquiries into this dark catastrophe, no doubt is entertained that the unfortunate girl was murdered in a moment of confiding affection by a monster - rather a demon - in the form of man, by whom she had become pregnant. The monument is of massive stone, extremely simple, but of conspicuous form and dimensions.'

Think about it. The whole community in which your family lives is absolutely convinced that you carried out a horrible crime. The report goes on:

> 'We subjoin a correct copy of the inscription, which has been attentively read many hundreds of times during the last three Sundays that have elapsed since its erection, Cadoxton churchyard now forming the favourite object of a walk to the inhabitants of the surrounding district.'

The report ends with the words of the inscription.

There was no getting away from it. The people knew, in their eyes beyond all reasonable doubt. Perhaps the family had a reputation. Perhaps Llewelyn had, and they wouldn't let it go.

On 16 April 1825 Llewelyn Richards was tried at the Glamorgan Great Sessions in Cardiff.

THE PRESSURE MUST HAVE BEEN HUGE. INTOLERABLE AND, AS THEY SAY, UNTENABLE

The indictment reads:

'Accused of murder by beating her and throwing her into a rivulet. The deceased was pregnant and the prisoner suspected of being the father. She used to be a servant of the prisoner's father.'

The prosecution was brought by her father. Llewelyn's plea was 'not guilty'.

The Cambrian newspaper described the imposing spectacle of the Great Sessions. There was 'a large party of the neighbouring nobility and gentry in carriages. The weather was very auspicious.' It then lists the cases and the verdicts and all it says is:

'Llewellyn Richards, charged with the murder of Margaret Williams, late of the parish of Cadoxton, was acquitted.'

Still there was no evidence. Suspicion, rumour and innuendo have never been sufficient.

But the pressure must have been huge. Intolerable and as they say, untenable.

Not long afterwards Llewelyn left Swansea on a cargo vessel to start a new life in America. But his family still had to face that eternal call for vengeance from the graveyard across the road, standing on the main path through the village for all to see, every day. There can be no wiping away of the crime whilst those words are set in stone. There is consolation that whilst he might escape human justice there must come an inescapable final reckoning. A greater power is in pursuit. Llewelyn might run - and we can be sure that he did - but he could never hide, and for some, in the anticipation of revenge there was hope.

The Murder Stone, so easily found, speaks of tragedy. It speaks of two families scarred. Of a life taken. Of lives ruined. It is a crime and pain that endures. There are still flowers placed on Margaret's grave. A grave that is incongruous amongst the records of ordinary lives that ran their course in this village - the Richards, the James, the Griffiths, the Owens. But this is different. This is a woman betrayed and murdered.

This is the local legend, the story that has endured, but perhaps there is a different story. You see, there is another version of these awful circumstances that may be just as compelling. It comes from a book by Charles Wilkins of Springfield, Merthyr, published in 1879, fifty years after these events. He says in his Preface that what he tells us is true.

In his version Llewelyn, who lived with his widowed mother, was indeed arrested and charged. A neighbour, Parry, claimed he had seen Llewelyn and Margaret together on the night of the murder, looking as if they had quarrelled. There was no other compelling evidence and so Llewelyn was released. However, local feeling ran high and Llewelyn and his mother were ostracised by the neighbours. It proved too much. His mother died and Llewelyn emigrated to Australia. But it was Parry who was the killer. He confessed on his deathbed. He had approached Margaret on the marsh and when his advances were rejected, he had attacked her. His accusation threw the scent off himself, but he couldn't make it stick. He'd done enough to point the finger, though in all honesty he didn't have to do much. Margaret

herself had already prepared the ground during her pregnancy. Everyone had already made their minds up. He himself was in the clear.

Did Charles Wilkins of Springfield Merthyr really know something? Did the true murderer frame the father of her unborn child? What did Llewelyn and Margaret talk about when they met on the marsh on Saturday night? Was it a planned meeting? Or a chance encounter? Is this cliché-ridden tale the truth? Or is it a romantic fiction based upon cheap novels, a recycled story?

Of course it brings us no closer to the truth. Nothing will now. All we know is that a pregnant woman was murdered. Her life and the potential of her child, snuffed out on a marsh. The passage of time has dissolved an outrage into a curiosity. But the stone is still there silently pointing, a symbol of divine pursuit.

But I now look at it with some sadness, for it is the stone and the power of Elijah Waring's words that are remembered today, rather than poor Margaret, found dead upon a marsh. &

Based upon an article that first appeared in Welsh Country magazine in Mar/Apr 2005

Margaret's murder stone sits prominently next to the path

THE MURDER STONE SPEAKS OF TRAGEDY, OF TWO FAMILIES SCARRED. OF A LIFE TAKEN. OF LIVES RUINED.

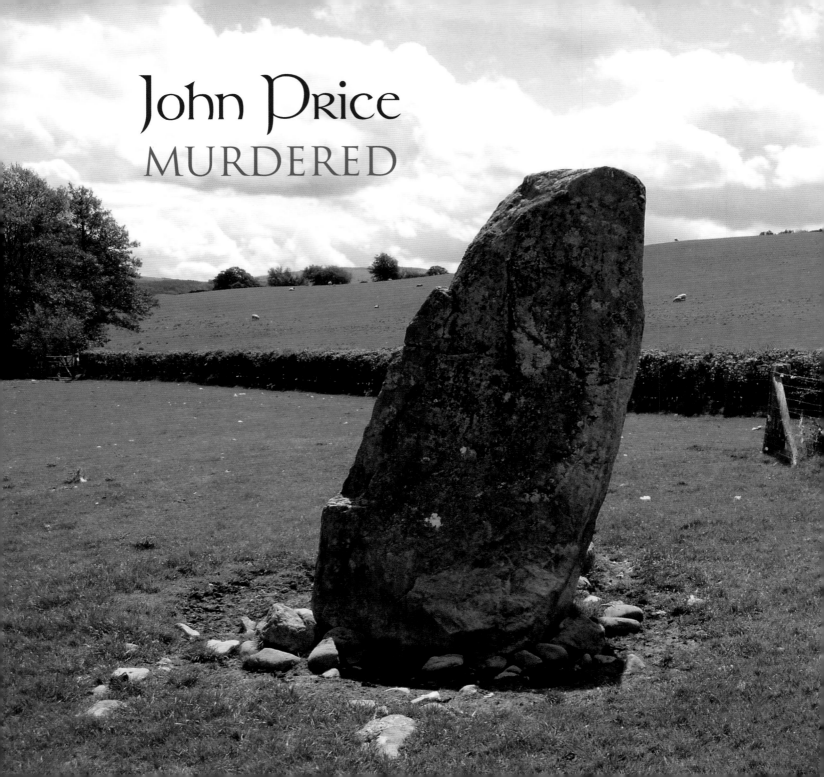

John Price
MURDERED

1826

LLANAFAN FAWR

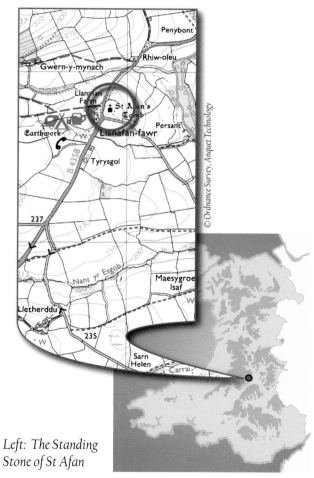

© Ordnance Survey, Anquet Technology

Left: The Standing Stone of St Afan

Take the B4358 from Beulah towards Newbridge on Wye. When you arrive in the village at the top of the hill park in front of the Red Lion public house.

The church is opposite. Enter the churchyard by the gate and approach the main door of the church. In front of you to the right, you will find the chest tomb of St. Afan. Then walk down the main path away from the church and you will find the grave of John Price about thirty yards along on the right. The inscription is faded but still discernable.

To find the standing stone where St. Afan was killed, drive down the narrow road by the side of the churchyard, which is signposted Cilmery. After about a mile you will come to the entrance to Dolyfelin Farm. You can park here with care. Walk down the drive and ask the residents for permission. The stone is a few hundred yards away on the right. Don't worry the sheep.

It is easy to miss the church that stands quietly in Llanafan Fawr. It is a fine church, peaceful and untouched. But it is not to be ignored.

It has a long history - and a murderous one. The churchyard at Llanafan Fawr contains one of the oldest living objects in the country and also another of our Murder Stones. It is a place that more than repays your attention. The Red Lion has a fine history book of the pub available for sale by the landlord, Adrian Foster. This tells you that its history can be dated at least as far back as 1189 when Geraldus Cambrensis slept here. You will be guided to stories of witchcraft, miracles and lost treasure. The church itself is built upon an Iron Age mound, but is pre-dated by the huge yew tree estimated to be over 2300 years old. It is a tree that has seen so much. All this drama. All this murder.

It begins with the death of St. Afan. You will find his tomb to the right of the porch, a large altar slab with faint Lombardic script. St. Afan is a mysterious figure. There is some dispute about his identity but he is most likely to have been the 10th century Bishop Jeuan who was bishop only for a day. He was killed defending Llanafan Fawr from a Viking raiding party in a meadow a mile or so behind the church, on Dolyfelin farm. The spot is marked by a large standing stone. It is so peaceful and quiet in the meadow and as you stand and look around, you will be struck by the remoteness and the beauty of where you are. Hills unchanged, kites circling as they always have. Down through the years a community has lived here and lives have been carved out, away from the rest of us. Jealousies, rivalries, disputes, vendettas - things that the rest of us have known nothing about - have consumed them, defining their lives and their deaths. Old rivalries. Old crimes. The descendants still live in the parish.

The Murder Stone, an old weathered stone, is almost indecipherable now. It looks out at an unchanged landscape, but tells us about a completely different time. In itself it is unique, for it carries upon it both the name of the victim and his murderer. If you stare at it long enough the inscription slowly emerges from the past:

John Price who was murdered on the Darren Hill in this parish by R. Lewis April 21 1826

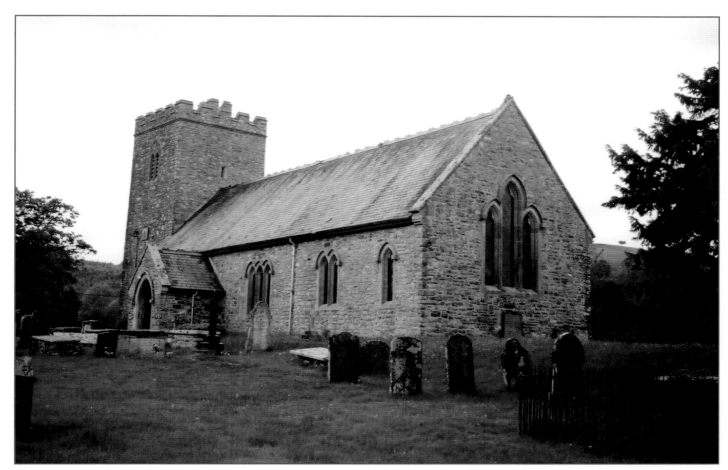

The churchyard at Llanafan Fawr

IT'S A FINE CHURCH, PEACEFUL AND UNTOUCHED; BUT IT IS NOT TO BE IGNORED

JOHN LEWIS WAS FRIGHTENED AND RESOLVED RATHER TO BE HANGED HERE THAN STARVED THERE

The Cambrian newspaper reported the murder a week later. It tells us that John Price was found,

> 'his neck twisted till the blood ran out of his ears so that his death must have been occasioned by a dislocation of his vertebrae.'

Suspicions fell upon Rees Lewis, a shepherd and neighbour who had disappeared. Lewis was a man with a vicious temper. They lived about three quarters of a mile apart and had fought and feuded constantly. But the Price family didn't need evidence. Their suspicions in all circumstances always fell upon the notorious Lewis family. This was one of the final acts in a tangled web of accusations, irritation, damage, theft and assaults that combined these two families in mutual loathing and which had sparked another notorious murder

John Price's gravestone

42 years previously, when Lewis Lewis killed Thomas Price. These same names run all the way through this murky story.

The Lewis family were, it seems, a lawless bunch. They were famous for it. They were described as 'a vicious, wicked set of people.' Sheep stealing, riotous behaviour and assault run like refrains through the history of the family. David Lewis was transported to Australia for stealing a turkey. His wife Margaret was accused of murdering an illegitimate infant son, conceived in David's absence; over 20 witnesses testified against her, but she still got off and went on to become the midwife in the parish. While sheep stealing appeared to be routine.

The Price family weren't much better. Thomas Price himself was accused of Riot and Assault in July 1784, just before his murder, and his relatives were involved in stealing livestock themselves. They had some way to go to match the Lewis family but they were trying their best. It is certainly the case that the two families didn't like each other. This one gravestone, commemorating a murder in 1826, represents a whole series of misdemeanours and deaths, each crime the justification for the next. There is a suggestion that the enmity arose originally in a dispute over property, but by 1784 the Lewis family were finding one Price in

particular, Thomas, hard to take. However bad they were, they regarded him as worse, 'a perfect villain.' They would often find their sheep dead in the fields, laid head to tail in a row, killed by Price and his dogs.

42 YEARS PREVIOUSLY, LEWIS LEWIS KILLED THOMAS PRICE; THE SAME NAMES RUN ALL THE WAY THROUGH THIS MURKY STORY

Then in October 1784 Thomas Price disappeared. A search was organised, a search that even involved one of the Lewis family, young Thomas Lewis, but there was no trace of Price or his dog. Obviously suspicions immediately fell upon the Lewis clan. They were accused by Thomas Price's wife Gwenllian, and four of them were taken before magistrates in Brecon, but there was no evidence. In spite of the offer of rewards, the trail went cold - but at least the Lewis sheep remained untroubled. However, the story would eventually unravel from an unexpected source.

Their offences continued to stack up for the next four years until John Lewis was convicted of sheep stealing in the Spring

They spent all night trying to burn a wet body using wood and turf

Sessions in 1788. He was sentenced to transportation for 14 years. The prospect was horrifying. A contemporary account tells us that he was 'frightened in the highest degree at the accounts from thence and resolved rather to be hanged here than to be starved there.' But there may have been an additional reason why he should so want to implicate his nearest and dearest. His brother David was also in prison and he was found in his cell in a compromising position with John's wife, making what was obviously a bit more than a social call. So he told the magistrates everything he knew about the death of Thomas Price, although he was not directly involved. He had also fallen out with his brother Lewis Lewis who was, by now, also imprisoned and awaiting transportation, and could see no reason to protect him or his two sons, one also called Lewis and the other Thomas.

So young Thomas Lewis was arrested and within a fortnight he turned King's Evidence and in so doing condemned both his father and his brother to the gallows. His story was a simple and macabre one.

Lewis Lewis the elder had had enough of his neighbour and so offered sheep to his boys if they would kill Thomas Price. Lewis Lewis the younger and his pal Evan Davies were quite keen to take up the offer, though Thomas claimed that he was less enthusiastic and that his brother Lewis made all the plans. In October 1784 the three of them waylaid Thomas Price near a house called Eskyr Nevill. Some brief words were exchanged and then they set upon him. Lewis knocked him to the ground with a stick and then strangled him, whilst Davies thumped him in the stomach. Thomas Lewis said that all he did was pull him down by his legs. Their indictment would later say that they 'did not have the fear of God before their eyes but (were) being moved and seduced by the instigation of the devil.'

Once he was dead, Lewis took Price's purse, later to share the contents of 6 shillings between them, and they threw the body into a pool. Lewis then took the dog away and hanged the spaniel with the cord that had strangled its master. Thomas Lewis was already regretting his involvement with his brother and so joined the search party to throw suspicion away from himself. Neither was he involved in the subsequent removal of the body to a deeper pool called Ferlen Fawr, where it was submerged with a large boulder.

Thomas was implicated however in May 1785, for it was he who found it when it came back up to the surface. So with the assistance of their father, the brothers put the corpse into a sack and carried it by horse to the house of Lewis Lewis the Younger in darkness.

They then spent all night trying to burn a wet body using wood and turf. They had to keep going outside to make sure that the smoke they generated - not to mention the smell - didn't attract the neighbours. A vain hope, but the neighbours believed that the 'horrid foul smell' indicated they were burning sheep skins. It was the sort of thing the Lewis family did. In the morning they packed up the bones yet unburnt and trampled the fragments and the ashes into the garden. The next night they had another go at the troublesome bones, this time at the home of Lewis Lewis the Elder, again scattering the debris into the garden the next morning. It was not a task they could ever perform efficiently and of course these fragments of bone in the garden would prove to be decisive evidence. They did indeed stamp upon the

skull, but the pieces were still recognisable 4 years later. Evan Davies and the younger Lewis fled once they realised that Thomas was in custody. Davies disappeared but Lewis was apprehended in Dolgellau. He was tried and condemned to death. He was reconciled with his brother Thomas and tried his best to exonerate his desperate father and the missing Davies, though to no effect.

A large crowd witnessed his execution,

Once he was dead, Lewis took Price's purse and they threw the body into a pool

the first in Brecon for 30 years. They gathered outside the gaol on the banks of the River Tarrell. Lewis' mother turned up to watch. It is reported that she was eating a pie. Her major concern appeared to be that he might further implicate his father in any final address he might make. She was heard to call out "Bydd farw'n galed Lewis." - 'Die hard Lewis.' All he chose to say as the cart moved away was "God have mercy on me." Otherwise you will no doubt be pleased to learn that it was an occasion of the 'greatest decorum and solemnity.' There was another such occasion two years later, when Lewis Lewis the Elder was eventually hanged.

The back of the church at Llanafan Fawr

ALL THAT PASSION AND HATRED - ONCE SO REAL - IS NOW REPRESENTED BY A SIMPLE CRUMBLING STONE

Vendettas have a habit of repeating themselves. So when Rees Lewis murdered John Price in 1826 he strangled him, this time with a necktie. He pleaded not guilty but to little avail. He was pronounced guilty and, like his relatives before, hanged at Brecon. He was the last of the family to be hanged and his reward for sustaining such a notable tradition was to be mentioned on John Price's gravestone in Llanafan Fawr. The Price family could not miss an opportunity to point a finger at their enemies through the gravestone, one which speaks of decades of mayhem. All that passion and hatred, once so real, is now represented by a simple crumbling stone.

On this occasion, other family traditions too had been preserved. Rees Lewis was accused of the murder along with his son David, but whilst they were under arrest the latter commented that he had seen blood on his father's shirt. It was this that eventually convicted him; comments from another member of the clan. This argument between Price and Lewis had started as yet another dispute about sheep. It ended with Price dead in a ditch. Price's son found him with a necktie pulled and knotted so tightly round his throat that he couldn't unfasten it.

When David Lewis was called to give evidence in court his mother and his father were seen to try to shut him up. Their attempts were squashed by the judge. Poor David was overawed and confused. He could neither read nor write and had never attended school. He faced the judge and answered questions simply. As he thus recounted what he had seen, all hope for his father disappeared. The key moment was when he described how he had seen blood on his father's face and that he had watched him clean it off with grass. The jury took fifteen minutes to reach a verdict of guilty. So Rees was executed in Brecon on 14 August 1826. He became one of the few murderers ever to be remembered by name on his victim's headstone.

But we can't find the grave of Lewis Lewis the younger, 'this man of whom his neighbours were in perpetual fear.' After his execution back in 1789, his body was displayed in a gibbet at Garth Hill, near Llanafan Fawr. The family took away his body for secret burial in the dead of night during a storm. Unable to release the ankle chains they cut off his feet and left them behind. A local dog found the feet and took one home to his master at Dolyfelin Farm. ☙

Based upon an article that first appeared in Welsh Country magazine in Sept/Oct 2005

Adeline Coquelin
DROWNED

1828

PEMBREY

© Ordnance Survey, Anquet Technology

Drive along the A484 out of Llanelli, heading for Kidwelly and Carmarthen. Go through Burry Port and on to Pembrey. As you drive through the village you will find St Iltyd's Church on the left. Immediately after the church take a sharp left turn which will take you to the back of the church where you can park easily. Enter the churchyard here and you will find the memorial stone up against the wall of the church. Napoleon's name stands out very clearly.

EACH WRECK WAS A TRAGEDY TO SOMEONE. BUT TO OTHERS IT WAS AN OPPORTUNITY

Cefn Sidan is the site of many shipwrecks. The bones of the ships are still there, though as the estuary re-shapes and reforms itself and the treacherous sands move, the wrecks shift. Famous landmarks on the move. These dunes are active.

The land juts out like a jaw, with the Gwendraeth estuary an open mouth ready to swallow the unwary. Stretching southwards towards Pembrey is a seven mile beach famous for land speed record attempts. In the background of the old photos of

SACRED

To the Memory of L! Col. Coquelin, aged 45 Years. And Adeline, his daughter aged 12Yr Both natives of France, who lost their lives by the wreck of the Ship "La Jeune Emma," on Cefn sidan Sand, as they were returning home from Martinique, in the West-Indies, and were interred in this ground on the 25th of Nov! 1828.

The above named Lady was Niece to Josephine, Consort of that renowned Individual. NAPOLEON BUONAPARTE.

The Captain, Chacelot de Chatillion, and five Seamen also perished in the same Shipwreck, and were buried near this place.

In Dec! 1833, was wrecked the Ship Brothers" of Liverpool from Bahia, on Cefn sidan Sand, which caused the death of five persons whose remains also lie buried here.

In July 1839, the Ship Pickering Dodge" of Boston, America was driven on the same Sand, by which several Seamen lost their lives. Thomas Sweet, Jacob Winters, & Luther Goldwright were buried in this ground.

For particulars see the Parish Registers.

Freespirit Images

182 VESSELS ARE RECORDED AS BEING WRECKED ON THIS STRETCH OF COASTLINE. EXPLOITING WRECKS WAS A WELCOME MEANS OF SUPPLEMENTING MEAGRE INCOMES

brave young men in crash helmets there are always rotting hulks, while at the northern end the word "Danger" is spread all over the Ordnance Survey Map.

Cefn Sidan. The Silken Back.

The geography of the area betrays the unwary. The estuary is a vast expanse of water, and unprepared sailors can fail to appreciate how shallow it is. Many have been caught out. On this stretch of coastline 182 vessels are recorded as being wrecked.

Each wreck was a tragedy to someone. But to others it was an opportunity.

Exploiting wrecks was a welcome means of supplementing meagre incomes when times were hard, as they often were, and the business needed a little boost. They were said to shine lights from their houses to entice shipping, perhaps even shining them from the church tower, deceiving sailors with the false hope of security.

The men of Pembrey were known as the 'Gwyr y Bwelli Bach' - the Men of the Small Hatchets. Perhaps they still are, though I hope not. It is a reference to the little axes they are said to have carried with them when they went out to wrecks. On one side the axe had a claw for ripping open any cargo or for prising away wood, a valuable commodity. The other side could always be employed

in helping the distressed or injured on their way, especially if they might be regarded as witnesses by unsympathetic authorities. But if they didn't need any such help, then the axe was useful for cutting off the swollen fingers of anyone wearing a valuable-looking ring.

Of course, the good people of Pembrey were not alone in their interest in this occasional harvest from the sea. In 1769 a French ship carrying rum and brandy capsized near Aberthaw. The story goes that about 2000 people gathered and set about

ON ONE SIDE THE AXE HAD A CLAW FOR RIPPING OPEN CARGO; THE OTHER SIDE COULD ALWAYS BE EMPLOYED TO HELP THE INJURED ON THEIR WAY

the wreck with hatchets and enthusiasm in order to save the cargo. They say that 35 people died on that beach from alcoholic poisoning and were buried where they fell. But of course there has never been very much else to do in Aberthaw.

ONE OF THE COFFINS WAS OPEN AND THE BODY WAS MISSING; ALL THAT REMAINED WAS A BLUE SHIRT

On Friday 21 November 1828 the French ship La Jeune Emma made a fatal error. She was sailing from Martinique to Le Havre with a cargo of rum, sugar, ginger, cotton and coffee and had had a difficult crossing. The ship had experienced severe weather throughout the crossing and the crew had been unable to take any accurate observations. Captain de Châtillon became disorientated in thick fog and mistook Land's End for Cape Finisterre and then the Lundy Island light for Ushant light, off the coast of Brittany. The design of the lighthouse on Lundy was partly to blame. It had two lights but from a distance they merged into one. So although he was in Carmarthen Bay, he believed he was looking at the single light of Ushant and sailed straight into Cefn Sidan.

The Carmarthen Journal tells us that:

'The whole of the crew and passengers which were below rushed up onto the deck, over which the sea broke frightfully and before daylight it appeared 13 souls had been swept away by the continual breaking of the sea and met a watery grave.'

Amongst them were Lieutenant-Colonel Coquelin and his 12 year old daughter Adeline, niece to Josephine de Beauharnais, the divorced wife of Napoleon, and their two servants.

Some of the crew eventually made it to shore on a makeshift raft and a local farmer swam his horse to the wreck to rescue another. It is reported that they received a 'most hospitable reception from the inhabitants.' Now they were out of the way they could get on with the proper business of salvage.

By noon on Saturday, news of the wreck had reached Carmarthen and the Militia set off to protect the cargo. They were too late. The wreckers had stripped the ship before the tide had changed. The Journal naturally was outraged. 'They are worse than the wild savages of America.'

Possibly so, but it would have been a strong willed man indeed who could have ignored such exotic and unexpected opportunities.

The bodies of Captain de Châtillon and Colonel Coquelin were washed ashore on the rocks on Sunday morning, along with the forlorn and battered body of 12 year old Adeline. The sea does not discriminate. The ship broke up that same morning, littering the coast with debris. It was all collected.

The French Consul came down for the burial in St. Iltyd's Church in Pembrey and poor Adeline was buried with her father. She was treated with dignity and reverence, unlike other victims of La Jeune Emma who were buried across the estuary in Laugharne. After a couple of days the surface of their grave appeared to have sunk. When the final body was washed up some time later, it was interred in the same grave. The reason for the subsidence became clear. One of the coffins was open and the body missing. All that remained was a blue shirt.

The reputation of the locals for lawlessness was as well documented as the tide. The stone in Pembrey goes on to refer to the loss of the ship "Brothers" from Bahia in 1833. As a result of this disaster, the magistrate J. H. Rees found himself in a bit of bother with the locals. In fact on Boxing Day he was sufficiently moved to write a letter to his bosses at the Home Office.

The ship was wrecked on 19 December 1833 and was carrying cotton and buffalo

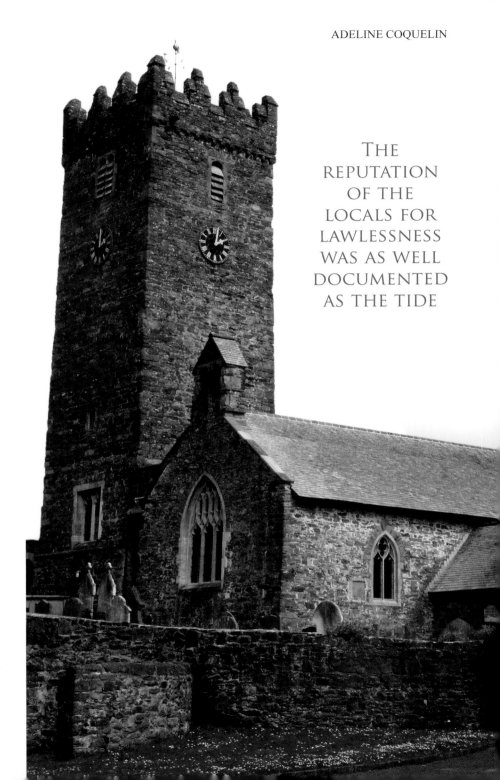

THE REPUTATION OF THE LOCALS FOR LAWLESSNESS WAS AS WELL DOCUMENTED AS THE TIDE

hides and horns to Liverpool. Of the crew of 16, only the carpenter survived.

THEY WERE COMING FROM AS FAR AWAY AS CARMARTHEN. THERE MUST HAVE BEEN QUITE A TRAFFIC JAM

The winds were strong and almost all of the cargo and the wreck itself were driven on shore between Kidwelly and Pembrey. When Mr. Rees arrived, it seemed to him that the whole population was busy in helping itself to the booty. Well, with Christmas coming up what did he expect? It was all being taken away in carts. They were coming from as far away as Carmarthen. There must have been quite a traffic jam. Masts were sawn up and bales of cotton carried away. He writes:

> 'I warned the people, many of whom were farmers of respectability, of the consequences of this proceeding but I did not succeed in deterring them from doing so. I have very highly to complain of the conduct of a gentleman who resided near in refusing me the assistance of his carts and men to preserve some of the goods.'

In the face of such riches his authority was meaningless, for he had no power to enforce it. When he wasn't ignored, he was assaulted. But what sort of man, alone, confronts two farm labourers chopping up a bowsprit on a beach and tells them they can't do it? Poor Mr. Rees. He wasn't at all sure what to do.

> 'As the number of offenders is so great and many of them of much respectability I should wish to have the honour of your Lordship's instructions on the subject. I venture to suggest that unless some examples be made, these disgraceful scenes will again occur as wreckers are frequently on this coast.'

Too true.

Wrecking may have been generally consigned to the past but boats are still lost in these dangerous waters. In 1996 an unnamed vessel was lost carrying almost £1 million worth of cannabis resin. The cargo might be different, but the threat of Cefn Sidan, the Silken Back, remains. ❧

Based upon an article that first appeared in Welsh Country magazine in July/Aug 2006

Cefn Sidan estuary from Burry Port

THE CARGO MIGHT BE DIFFERENT, BUT THE THREAT OF CEFN SIDAN, THE SILKEN BACK, REMAINS

Mary Kavanagh
MURDERED

1829

PENRICE

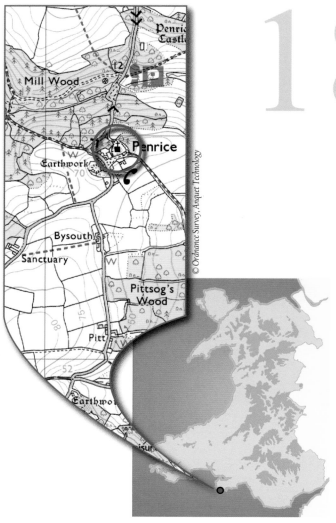

© Ordnance Survey, Anquet Technology

Drive along the A4118 out of Swansea towards Port Eynon. After the turning to Oxwich you must take the next road on the left that is signposted "Penrice".

Follow this narrow road, which falls sharply and then rises again into the village. There is room to park immediately in front of St. Andrew's Church. You will find the grave on the left hand side of the church, a short distance from the door.

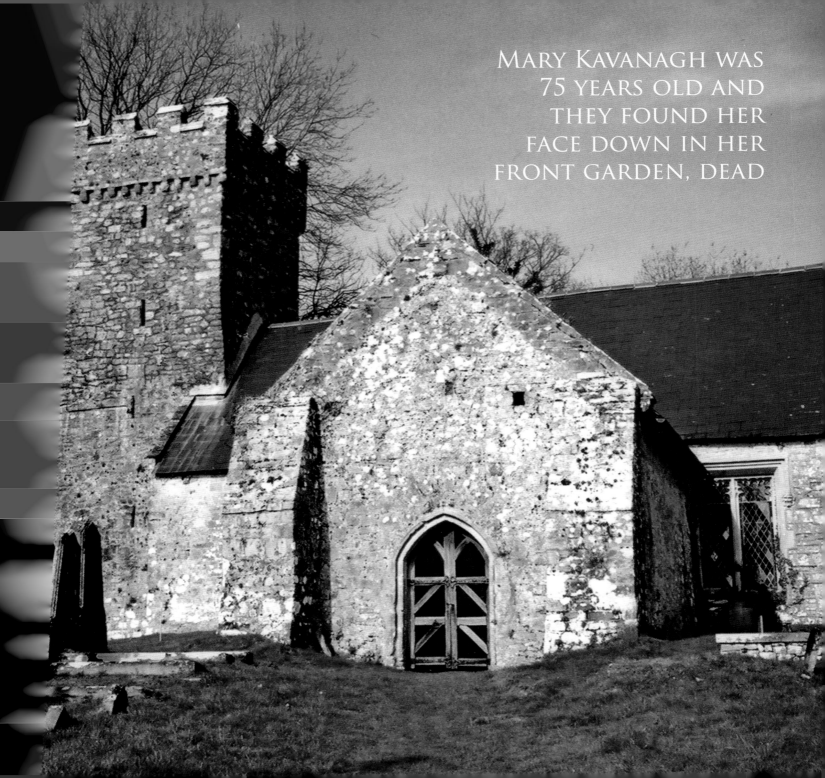

MARY KAVANAGH WAS 75 YEARS OLD AND THEY FOUND HER FACE DOWN IN HER FRONT GARDEN, DEAD

Freespirit Images

'IT IS CONJECTURED THAT THE WRETCH WHO COMMITTED
THE DEED HAS NOT OBTAINED ANYTHING OF MUCH VALUE'

Mary Kavanagh was 75 years old and they found her face down in her front garden, dead, with her head smashed in. It was Tuesday morning, 6 October 1829.

The last time she had been seen alive was on Saturday evening at about 5 o'clock in her cottage in Penmaen, Gower. On Sunday, the neighbours noticed that the curtains were drawn and they remained so on Monday. They were not too concerned because they thought she'd gone away as she sometimes did. No one thought to go into the garden.

However on Tuesday, two female neighbours, 'fearing that the deceased might have died suddenly,' went to have a look. They climbed over the garden wall and found Mary lying near her front door.

The report in The Cambrian, four days later, explores the particulars of the death in close detail. But even after all these years the brutality of the murder still has the power to shock. The paper takes an almost prurient pleasure in describing her condition.

Her body was facing the door with her hands underneath. The head 'was very bloody' and there was 'a frightful wound on the back part of the head.' She had been hit twice from the left side by a blunt instrument and 'part of the bone was beaten into the brain.' Blood had flowed 'nearly three yards from the body.' A 'considerable portion of the brain was found lodged' in her cap.

It was clearly a burglary and the details of the 'small round table near the fireplace upon which a Testament was lying open and a pair of spectacles on it,' establish her credentials as a pious widow, set upon by murderous vagabonds.

Something had drawn her into the garden, for her key was in the lock on the inside of the door. The larger drawers of her chest were opened and their contents appeared to have been ransacked. The smaller drawers were on the floor. On the chest there was a candlestick with the candle half burnt and the wick blown out, and the iron handle of a fire shovel by which the lock of one of the drawers appeared to have been forced.

Coroner Charles Collins and the jury searched the room. There was a large oak chest that was still locked and contained

'seven sovereigns, a Bank of England note for £20 and securities for several sums of money, amounting to £120.'

All that was missing was a couple of watches that Mary had hung over the mantelpiece.

MUCH BETTER
TO BELIEVE THAT
CRIME WAS THE
RESPONSIBILITY
OF STRANGERS,
NOT SOMEONE
YOU LIVED WITH

'It is conjectured that the wretch
who committed the horrid deed
has not obtained any thing of much
value.'

Poor Mary. Drawn outside and attacked.
Then a frantic cursory search, adrenaline
pumping. No time to waste, not with a body in
the garden. The savings accumulated over 75
hard years were left in an oak chest and Mary
was left murdered in the garden.

Murdered for watches.

THE CRIME WAS NEVER SOLVED

There were rumours enough, naturally, but
the paper adopts a lofty tone.

'For the needs of justice we abstain
from noticing the various rumours in
circulation relating to this foul deed.'

This, though, was a small community, a
scattered village across a hilltop above the sea.
Anonymity was difficult, almost impossible,
to achieve. Everyone knew everyone else.
Much better to believe that crime was the
responsibility of strangers - travellers, beggars,
pedlars - not committed by someone you
lived with. Itinerants to whom they closed
their doors, who they watched walking
down the lanes - perhaps they were the ones
who had found an old lady alone, easy meat.
Was it a moment of casual opportunism? A
more comfortable idea than to think she was
watched closely over a period of time and

beaten to death by someone who believed she had riches hidden in her cottage. Someone you saw every day.

The crime was never solved.

When the gravestone was erected in the churchyard of St. Andrew's, Penrice, perhaps as much as a year after the murder, there was nothing to put upon it to bring about closure. A brutal unsolved murder. The gibbet that once stood a mile away at Hangman's Cross remained unused.

You will find the gravestone if you follow the narrow lanes that lead to Penrice, tucked in behind the Penrice Estate. It is a hidden village that is today peaceful and isolated. Once it was a centre of commerce, the site of two weekly markets and four annual fairs. There is still the Crying Stone on the green where their opening would be announced. A notable place for prize-fighting. Now all that is left is a memory of brutal violence, in a quiet neat churchyard. The limestone on the grave has been eroded, eaten away by the winds from Oxwich Bay down below. It is very hard to read:

> *To the memory of Mary, wife*
> *of James Kavanagh of Penmaen,*
> *who was murdered.*

The rest may have disappeared but the word "murdered" still stands out, on this ordinary stone to the left of the church porch. A shocking intrusion into ordinary lives.

The world of course went on. A rural murder would live on in the minds of the villagers, but not so long for anyone else. The Cambrian carries an invitation to tender for the design of a Clifton Suspension Bridge. Seven reindeer are for sale, a valuable acquisition for a gentleman's park. A man was arrested for laughing at a policeman.

But no one was ever arrested for the murder of Mary Kavanagh. ❧

Based upon an article that first appeared in Welsh Country magazine in July/Aug 2005

St. Andrew's Church, Penrice

NOW ALL THAT IS LEFT IS A MEMORY OF BRUTAL VIOLENCE, IN A QUIET NEAT CHURCHYARD

Richard Lewis
EXECUTED

1831

ABERAFAN

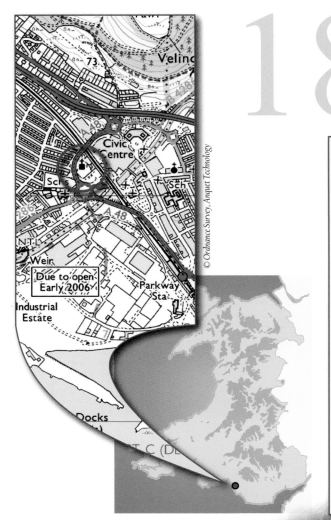

© Ordnance Survey, Anquet Technology

Drive to the centre of Port Talbot and look for the bus station. Immediately opposite the bus station you will see St. Mary's Church. You can park in front of the church in a pay and display car park. Walk down the central path through the churchyard. Just before you reach the centre — and thus the church — you will find the grave of Richard Lewis on the left hand side.

Richard Lewis was an innocent man. Everyone said so. Even the judge who condemned him said he was innocent. But he was still hanged and in his horrible death he became a symbol - a victim of oppression and of judicial murder.

A rallying cry for the Welsh working class. Richard Lewis. But call him Dic Penderyn.

St. Mary's church is in the heart of Port Talbot, nestling up against the fly-over. Richard's grave is marked by a simple Celtic cross and at the base of the cross, the equally simple inscription reads:

> *To the memory of*
> *Richard Lewis*
> *Executed at Cardiff*
> *For the part he played*
> *During the Industrial*
> *Riots in Merthyr Tydfil*
> *In June 1831*
> *Buried on 14 August*
> *1831 Aged 23 years*

There were flowers on his grave when I went to visit. Fading flowers perhaps, but they were a reminder of the enduring nature of the story of Dic Penderyn's tragic death. He has remained a vitally important figure in the history of the working class because of what happened to him. It is not really because of what he said or did, or for the ideas that he had. His importance rests almost entirely upon what they did to him.

You look at his grave in the certain knowledge that he stopped being an individual and became a representative of something much wider - the struggle of the working class against abuse and exploitation. For that's the whole point really. He became a symbol; he was targeted and killed by the authorities in his life and he was lionised by the rest in his death. They may have killed him, but they couldn't kill the ideas and beliefs that he represented. As a consequence, he has been a focal point for socialism and radicalism for almost two hundred years now. Yet, as always, behind all this there was a real person, who lived and loved, with no expectation of enduring martyrdom and fame. Although it is in the name of Dic Penderyn that he has been remembered, he was born Richard Lewis in 1808.

He was born in the parish of Pyle and was fortunate enough to receive some basic education in chapel, learning to read and write. In 1819 the family moved to Merthyr

77

A CALF WAS KILLED AND A WHITE CLOTH WAS DIPPED IN ITS BLOOD. THIS WAS RAISED AS A FLAG, A SYMBOL OF REBELLION

and he became a miner, like his father. Lots of things have been said about Dic Penderyn and, as an ordinary man, much of his life story remains unknown. It is said that he became radicalised and earned such a reputation as a defender of workers' rights that he was sacked when he was still only 15.

He was a highly regarded figure. He was physically impressive at a time when many were under-nourished; he was knowledgeable and a literate and impressive public speaker. Dic was a Welsh speaker and could move confidently throughout the multicultural mix of Merthyr at that time. He undoubtedly had natural leadership qualities and in fact, on one occasion, was sent to negotiate with the Merthyr ironmasters.

It is clear to us now that, sadly, this reputation sealed his fate. Unknown to himself, he was destined to become a scapegoat for the ruling classes when they were ready to re-assert their dominance. By 1831 he was working once more as a miner. He was married and his wife was

pregnant. An ordinary man, with ordinary responsibilities, facing an extraordinary future.

Things were not happy in Merthyr at this time. But then why should they ever have been any different? The conditions in which people lived and worked were truly awful. People had been drawn there by the availability of work. High wages were possible, particularly when compared with wages out in the country, but living conditions were squalid. Housing was poor. Disease was rife. Sanitary arrangements were often non-existent.

When the market for iron slumped in 1829 it was the workers who bore the brunt. Dismissal and redundancy, wage reductions, short term working. Add to this rising prices and you can have some idea of how hard the recession hit those who were already living hand to mouth in shocking conditions. While all the time the huge gulf between the rich and the poor continued to expand and of course, the Ironmasters who owned the industry controlled not just the economic power, but political power too. Workers worked, suffered and died. There had to be more to life than that.

On the 30 May there was a public meeting in Hirwaun on the topic of Parliamentary reform. The agenda however soon shifted. People there had more immediate concerns. A particular grievance was the Court of Requests, which dealt with the recovery of small debts, and the behaviour of the bailiffs who were repossessing what little property some of them had. It was clear that in the economic climate feelings were running high. Matters came to a head the following day. Bailiffs arrived at the home of Lewis Lewis near Merthyr, with the intention of seizing a cart. They were confronted by Lewis and his neighbours and although the bailiffs eventually took possession of a small trunk, a mob formed and marched on Hirwaun where they took it back from the shopkeeper to whom it had been given. The Merthyr Rising, the greatest uprising in Wales since the days of Owain Glyndwr, had begun.

A calf was killed and a white cloth was dipped in its blood. This was raised as a flag, perhaps the first time a red flag was used as a symbol of popular rebellion. A loaf of bread was impaled on a pole to represent the needs of the workers. They marched on Merthyr, ransacking houses and returning previously dispossessed property to its original owners. Shops were attacked and destroyed. Finally the home of the President of the Court of Requests, Joseph Cotton, was attacked and his furniture was destroyed. The High Sheriff called in the troops.

IT IS CLEAR TO US NOW THAT HIS REPUTATION SEALED HIS FATE

On the morning of Friday 3 June 1831 soldiers of the 93rd Highland Regiment, who had been based in Brecon, confronted a large and angry crowd of over 2000 people outside the Castle Inn in Merthyr. The Riot Act was read in both English and Welsh. The mob refused to disperse and, incited by Lewis Lewis, started to surround the soldiers outside the Inn in an attempt to seize their muskets. There was a scuffle. The soldiers from inside the building fired on the crowd. At least 16 people were killed, some say as many as 26. No soldiers were killed, though one, Donald Black, was wounded when he was stabbed by a bayonet in the thigh. The soldiers, facing a town in uproar and on the brink of revolt, retreated to await reinforcements.

79

The rioters had control of the town and a mob managed to intercept a force of Yeomen who had been sent from Swansea. An ammunition party from Brecon was waylaid. Law and order were clearly in danger of breaking down entirely. More workers arrived to join the uprising from the Monmouthshire ironworks. There was a whiff of revolution in the air. The troops were confronted once more, this time at Twyn y Waun. The Riot Act was read out once again and muskets were levelled. There was a tense moment of confrontation. But the events in front of the Castle Inn had had their influence. The workers began to disperse.

AN AMMUNITION PARTY WAS WAYLAID. LAW AND ORDER WERE CLEARLY IN DANGER OF BREAKING DOWN ENTIRELY

After 6 days the uprising was over. Order could slowly be restored. That indefinable moment of rebellion and revolution had passed, but its memory needed to be squashed. An example needed to be made. The workers needed to know their place; the possibility of further trouble needed to be removed. Supposed ring leaders were rounded up. There were mass arrests and imprisonment. One of those arrested was Dic Penderyn.

He was charged with riotously assembling at Merthyr Tydfil and feloniously attacking and wounding Donald Black of the 93rd Regiment while in the execution of his duties. He was tried at Cardiff Assizes and on the evidence of a tailor and a hairdresser, both from Merthyr, was found guilty and condemned to death. No one believed that Dic Penderyn had wounded Donald Black. Even the victim was unable to say that he had done it. He remembered seeing him in the crowd but that was all. There is no record of Dic Penderyn doing anything significant at all. All the judge could say was, "It is upon your head that the responsibility must rest for the blood which has fallen."

Lewis Lewis, who had been there at the very start of the trouble, was also condemned to death but his sentence was commuted to transportation for life to New South Wales. This was largely because of the evidence of a Special Constable John Thomas who testified that Lewis had saved him by putting himself between Thomas and enraged rioters.

But the sentence on Dic Penderyn was not commuted. His execution was set for 31 July. A petition was drawn up for a reprieve, supported, it was said, by 11,000 signatures. Notable figures spoke out against

Richard Lewis was hanged on St. Mary's Street, Cardiff on 13th August 1831

Dewi Bowen

Dewi Bowen

Riots in Merthyr Tydfil, 1831

the sentence. Even the judge who sentenced him, Justice Bosanquet, said he should be reprieved. William Crawshay the Iron master of Cyfarthfa paid for an appeal. The philanthropist Joseph Price of Neath was convinced of his innocence. There was, after all, no evidence that Dic Penderyn had played any significant part in any of the events of those six momentous days. He met with the Home Secretary, Lord Melbourne. A stay of execution was granted for two weeks, but at the end of that time he still saw no reason to change the verdict. There was nowhere else to go.

Richard Lewis, Dic Penderyn, was publicly executed.

A symbol that order had been restored once more? Or a scapegoat, hanged on the gallows in St. Mary's Street in Cardiff on 13 August 1831? Today we look at it and see his death as completely unjustifiable. Not an execution, but murder. He died proclaiming the injustice of his death.

"I am going to suffer unjustly. God, who knows all things, knows it is so. O Arglwydd, dyma ganwedd! (Oh Lord, here is injustice!)"

It was not an easy death. When the trap opened, his foot caught on the scaffold and Dic Penderyn was seen struggling. His executioner had to pull on his feet for several minutes until he could be declared to be dead.

His funeral procession through the Vale of Glamorgan became a considerable gathering and he was buried in the churchyard of St. Mary's in Port Talbot. The crowd that gathered outside the cemetery wall was addressed by Dic's brother in law, the

RICHARD LEWIS, DIC PENDERYN, WAS PUBLICLY EXECUTED. HE DIED PROCLAIMING THE INJUSTICE OF HIS DEATH

Reverend Morgan Howells. It was absolutely clear from now on who were the oppressors and who were the oppressed. Yes, they may have killed Dic Penderyn, but they could not quell the sense of outrage that was felt. Over the years that outrage has not dimmed, so that even today people still leave flowers on his grave.

There is a plaque outside the library in Merthyr Tydfil that refers to him as a martyr of the working class. In his cruel death he has undoubtedly achieved a kind of immortality. The struggle he came to represent continued. But I suspect that like most of us, he would much rather have been remembered for being a kind and loving husband and father. &

Eleanor Williams
MURDERED

At junction 46 of the M4 (Morriston Hospital, Swansea North, Llangyfelach) follow signs for Felindre. It is about 2 miles. When you arrive in the village take the turning to the right which is by the side of the old mill. The road is signposted to Garnswllt. It is very steep and almost immediately you must turn right again so that you are now behind the mill. You can park outside the Nebo Independent Chapel or a little bit further along the road, near the school. Go behind the chapel and you will find Eleanor's grave on the far right, leaning against the wall of the cemetery.

1832
FELINDRE

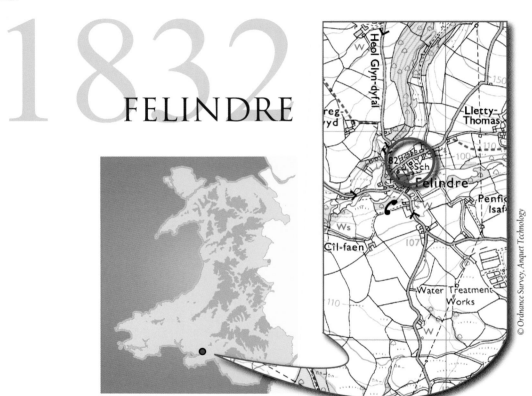

© Ordnance Survey, Anquet Technology

SUCH A DARK NIGHT. SUCH A LONG NIGHT. SUCH AN ISOLATED SPOT

The similarities between the Felindre Stone and the one in Cadoxton are striking. Two young women, both called Williams, both country girls from Carmarthenshire, working in service. Their deaths happened on estates owned by the same landowner, John Dillwyn Llewelyn. Both were killed on a Saturday night, during weekends when the winds were high.

Both were pregnant.

The Felindre Stone reads:

1832
To Record Murder
This stone was erected by general
subscription over the
Body of Eleanor Williams aged 29 years
A native of Carmarthenshire living in
service in this hamlet of Llangyfelach
With marks of violence upon her person
she was found dead in a well
By Llwyngwenno Farmhouse then in the
occupation of Thomas Thomas on the
morning of Sunday December the 9 1832
Although
The Savage Murderer may escape for a

season the detection of Man yet
Doubtless God hath set His mark upon
him either for time or eternity
And
The cry of blood will assuredly pursue
him to a terrible and righteous judgement.

Poor Eleanor's death received much less coverage than Margaret's though, because The Cambrian paper was full of General Election news at the time. There had been a shift in the state of the nation, so how could the fate of a humble servant girl compete? We are told about the great and the good, their speeches, the congratulations. Politics is suddenly everything. The Reform Act had been enacted and the number of Welsh parliamentary seats had increased from 27 to 32. This is a time of great change. The Cambrian says, 'It is rumoured that a great number of disorderly persons have got into the new parliament.'

Someone far more 'disorderly' was loose in Felindre. As if to underline the importance of parliamentary events, a comet was seen low in the sky. Earth tremors were felt in Neath. Such portents for a time of great change. The political landscape would never be the same again.

But then neither would Eleanor. Her life ended down a well on a farm, whilst her betters troubled themselves with celebratory dinners.

By the time her death is reported two weeks later, she gets no more than a few column inches. The paper confirms that on 9 December 1832 she was found dead in a well near Llwyngwenno Farmhouse. Such a dark night. Such a long night. Such an isolated spot. It would be no surprise if nothing had been seen or heard. There is still something about that image that disturbs - a woman thrown into a dark hole. Was her body battered by this action? Or was she already dead? The evidence is not clear. The report says that she had been beaten and killed, her skull fractured and her body had on it 'other marks of violence'. There was a 'patient investigation' by the Coroner Charles Collins, Esq. and the verdict reached was one of 'wilful murder against some person or persons unknown'. There are rumours surrounding the death, of course; it was a very small community after all. But the paper refuses to speculate:

'Several suspicious circumstances have however transpired which it is not thought to be prudent at present to publish'.

Such reticence. Their belief is that 'every exertion is made in the neighbourhood to bring the foul assassin to justice.' The Cambrian is convinced it is only a matter of time before an arrest is made. Of course their hopes were misplaced. No arrest was ever made. A collection was made to erect the gravestone, one which the landowner

Eleanor's gravestone can be found behind Nebo Chapel

THERE ARE RUMOURS SURROUNDING THE DEATH, OF COURSE; IT WAS, AFTER ALL, A VERY SMALL COMMUNITY

Llwyngwenno Farm. Eleanor's body was found in a well close to the farmhouse

SUCH A DARK NIGHT. SUCH A LONG NIGHT. SUCH AN ISOLATED SPOT. IT WOULD BE NO SURPRISE IF NOTHING HAD BEEN SEEN OR HEARD

supported. After all, John Dillwyn Llewelyn not only owned the Llangyfelach estate, he also owned the land where Margaret Williams had died in Neath. This might explain why the words on the stone parallel so closely those in Cadoxton. But there is a new poignant detail here. Now almost lost in the ragged uneven grass in front of the grave, you will find a small stone, representing Eleanor's unborn child.

A community did its best. Did its duty. But the words at the bottom of the stone acknowledge that the human endeavour had been unsuccessful. As in Cadoxton, they must wait for the Divine Justice that will surely run its course. It will come. Eventually.

If you believe, then it brings some consolation. Under the rough grass at the bottom of the stone there is the faintest memory of the famous quotation from Romans 12 Verse 19, here in Welsh:

> *'Beloved, never avenge yourself but leave it to the wrath of God, for it is written, Vengeance is mine, I will repay, says the Lord.'*

The stone, carved injudiciously in limestone, leans forlornly against the west wall, above the old mill. The words, eroded and almost indecipherable now, speak of vengeance and retribution. But it is an admission of failure. God's agents in this world have failed. Now it is up to Him.

We owe it to Eleanor to remember what little it is that we now know, but what we do know provokes a stream of questions. What events preceded her death? Who had she met? Was it a chance encounter with 'ratcatchers', whose appearance in the area so exercised the newspaper? Obviously you can't trust strangers. Or was it a planned meeting with a lover? Why else would she be outside? Why does the stone carry two names? Eleanor and the name of the tenant farmer Thomas Thomas? Why is this name so important? Why is the name of the farm alone considered insufficient? Is this a veiled accusation? Was he the subject of the rumours referred to in The Cambrian? Was her pregnancy the motive for her murder? Or an awful coincidence?

The winter nights were dark. They were long and women were vulnerable.

Someone did it. Someone's son, or father, or brother. But we know as much as we will ever know. All we have now are unanswerable questions. The stone is so degraded that it really seems to come from another time, lost and mossed in the corner of a chapel graveyard. As Eleanor's headstone gradually crumbles and fades in the weather, so she is slowly consigned to a forgotten history. &

Based upon an article that first appeared in Welsh Country magazine in May/Jun 2005

Jane Lewis
MURDERED?

1862

TONYREFAIL

A DAUGHTER
MURDERED.
HOW ISAAC
AND SELINA
MUST HAVE
PRAYED FOR
JUSTICE

© Ordnance Survey, Anquet Technology

You need to leave Tonyrefail town centre along Waunrhydd Road. Park where you can at the very end of Waunrhydd Road where it meets the A4093.

Next to the Working Men's Club you will see a children's playground. Behind the playground you will see a row of grave stones recovered and re-sited from the original cemetery. Jane's grave is lying close to these in the grass, along with those of other members of her family and the headstone of Aenon Chapel itself.

Let us start at the very end of the story with this poignant epitaph on a neglected, fallen gravestone in Tonyrefail.

In memory of Jane, daughter of ISAAC and SELINA LEWIS late of Tyn Coed in the parish of Llanillid who, on the Lord's Day December 2nd 1862 probably fell by cruel hand on Ty'n Tyle farm in the parish of Ystradfodwg: aged 23 years and though her blood is hitherto unavenged attention is directed to the day when light will have shon on the mysterious occurrence and guilt will be accorded its just reward.

A daughter murdered. How Isaac and Selina must have prayed for justice. This is a story that begins, as it often does, with an unmarried woman out alone. A cold dark afternoon near Tyntila in the Rhondda. An afternoon that ended in a death that is still shrouded in mystery. Never really solved. Always questioned. The death of Jane Lewis.

About half a mile above the village of Gellidawel in the Rhondda Valley there was Tyntila Farm. It was on the steep slope of Penrhys Mountain. The farm was occupied by Thomas and Maria Williams with their six children and, more importantly, by three servants. David Morgan was 15 years old, Thomas Edmunds was 26 and Jane Lewis, the niece of Maria, was 22.

On this Sunday afternoon Thomas Williams went off with his brother to visit a neighbouring farm before going to the Nebo Chapel in Heol Fach for the evening service. Maria stayed behind to look after the children. Edmunds left later on, also for the same chapel. Then Jane left half an hour later. She too was going to the Nebo Chapel. There she had arranged to meet her 'sweetheart' also called Thomas Williams, although he was known locally as Thomas Screens.

There you have it. All the important characters in this unhappy tale. The chronology of everyone's comings and goings confirmed by Maria who didn't go anywhere. Despite this, the sequence of events has never been fully untangled. Yes, murders are sometimes committed by strangers, but in most cases the victim knows their killer, often intimately. Was this murder any different? No one ever felt that there was any need to look for anyone else in connection with Jane's death.

When Uncle Thomas returned home he told Maria that he hadn't seen Jane at the service. Then Tom Screens turned up,

YES,
MURDERS
ARE
SOMETIMES
COMMITTED
BY
STRANGERS,
BUT IN
MOST CASES
THE VICTIM
KNOWS
THEIR
KILLER,
OFTEN
INTIMATELY.

WAS THIS
MURDER ANY
DIFFERENT?

Freespirit Images

SO EVERYTHING WAS IN PLACE. MURDER WEAPON
IDENTIFIED, POSSIBLE MOTIVE ESTABLISHED, AND
OPPORTUNITY CLEARLY AVAILABLE

worried that she wasn't there. His concern was that she had found another boyfriend. Perhaps significantly, he had come to the farm the long way round. There were two possible routes and he took the longer one. He also went away on that route too. Initially there was little concern for her, since they believed that she might have gone to a tea party in Gellidawel. But when she still didn't return Uncle Thomas and Edmunds took a lantern and went out to look for her. They didn't have to go very far. They first examined the outhouses and then dropped down towards Gellidawel along the shortest route. They soon found Jane, less than 200 yards from the house, close to a stile.

They immediately ran off to get the constable, Richard Wise, and a doctor, though there was no help that the latter could have offered. Her throat had been slashed open with a razor. There were three separate wounds.

At the Inquest PC Wise reported:

'I found a razor with blood on it 2 feet 7 inches from the body. A brooch untouched by her blood was 4 feet 1 inch from the body. A bonnet, ribbon and collar were 5 feet 6 inches from the body. There was blood on the bonnet and the ribbon. I noticed that the collar was cut in two and quite saturated with blood. The string of the bonnet was cut through.'

There was no sign of any struggle. The most logical explanation would be that she was attacked from behind. There is a contemporary report claiming that parts of her fingers were found attached to the razor, suggesting obviously that she had tried to fight off an attacker. However, the information that I write here comes from police reports and there is no suggestion of this significant detail in anything that they write. Apart from huge trauma to the neck, every other part of her appeared intact.

The razor had been identified. It belonged to Edmunds and was missing from its usual place on top of a cupboard back at the farm. It had been there on Sunday morning.

This was a vital piece of evidence. It reduced the possible suspects to a very small group indeed, unless there was some sort of highly elaborate conspiracy involving two razors.

Then, of course there was the post-mortem evidence that suddenly produced more crucial evidence and a possible motive.

Jane Lewis was 10 weeks pregnant.

Now you can see how things had started to stack up. You can see where the finger was pointing.

COULD ANYONE EVER DRAW A BLADE ACROSS THEIR OWN THROAT WITH SUCH DETERMINATION? JANE'S HEAD HAD NEARLY BEEN CUT OFF FOR GOODNESS SAKE

The surgeon also ruled out suicide. It was impossible for such wounds to be self-inflicted.

So everything was in place. Murder weapon identified, possible motive established, and opportunity clearly available. But after this, everything started to get rather muddy. In the first place PC Wise had already examined every article of clothing belonging to Edmunds. Not one drop of blood anywhere - and there would have been plenty. Neither could they place him in the vicinity of the crime at that particular time. So if it wasn't him then the only other person who could have done it was Tom Screens. There was the business about the route Screens had taken. He couldn't explain why he'd taken the longer route to the farm. Surely if he had been that concerned, he would have either been anxious to get there quickly, or he would have gone one way and then returned via the other. Everything suggested that he should be the number one suspect.

Except there were plenty of witnesses who could testify that he hadn't left the village until after chapel.

So the police arrested Edmunds and charged him with murder. Edmunds then admitted two things, one that the razor was his and two that he had achieved 'intimacy' with Jane about a month previously. No wonder Thomas Screens was concerned that she'd found another boyfriend. It was, however, a rather speculative arrest. There was no evidence against him at all. All the police had to go on was a lack of evidence against anyone else.

Edmunds had also been seen in the village before the chapel service. His alibi was as sound as that of Screens. Yes, the razor was his but that didn't prove that he had used it. It didn't prove that he had crept up behind Jane, pulled her head back and slashed at her throat three times. In fact, Edmunds had a pistol. So if he'd planned murder then why hadn't he used that and so distanced himself from any incriminating evidence? The razor, if anything, pointed to his innocence because there was also this issue of the absence of blood stains. It was all very strange. Furthermore, whilst he could possibly have had a motive, thinking perhaps that she was carrying his child, on that Sunday he had made enquiries about the possibility of obtaining a special marriage licence for himself and Jane.

Genuine? Or a red herring?

In the end none of it added up. There were two prime suspects, both with possible motives and both with cast-iron alibis. The police couldn't pin it on either of them. There wasn't quite enough evidence and so the inquest concluded that Jane Lewis had committed suicide. 'Suicide committed under temporary insanity' is what they said.

The local press were astounded. It was a verdict that to them defied all logic. How could a jury have overturned the advice of the medical profession that such injuries could not have been self inflicted? How could a young woman possibly have done what she did to herself? Could anyone ever draw a blade across their own throat with such determination? Jane's head had nearly been cut off for goodness sake.

There was a flurry of letters in the press. A member of the jury was driven to write in response to the 'Star of Gwent.'

'I have not the least doubt that Jane Lewis committed the awful and horrible deed upon herself.'

They couldn't pin the murder on Edmunds. He was in company, in the village, from 5.30 pm and Jane was murdered at about 6.00 pm.

In addition, the jury had been told that Jane had been crying and complaining about feeling unwell. She had been threatening to 'destroy herself.'

'If all this and the fact of her never having been of a very cheerful spirit does not prove despondency, what does? Is it not the most natural conclusion that the girl had determined to put an end to her own life and had carried the thought into action in the most determined manner?'

If this is true, then Jane was really determined to bring an end to everything. It is said that suicides need three attempts to cut themselves before they find either the desperation or the courage to go deep enough. If this is the case then on the third stroke Jane certainly did find the strength to get herself out of what may have been an impossible position.

What do I think? That Thomas Screens did it and that he tried to incriminate Edmunds by planting the razor that he had stolen either before or after the murder? Who knows what conversations went on between Jane and Screens? What did he believe? Had she told him about Edmunds? Had he heard about marriage plans? Was he angry? Betrayed? Trapped? Vengeful?

Obviously her parents could not believe a verdict of suicide. How could their daughter have done what she was alleged to have done? How could the little girl they had brought up have cut through her own throat almost to the spine? It must have made absolutely no sense. Hence the headstone, which tells us that she, was 'probably felled by a cruel hand' and which says, hopefully, that 'guilt will be accorded its just reward.'

They buried her on the western side of Aenon Baptist Chapel, Tonyrefail. She was the first person to be laid to rest in this cemetery, an honour that perhaps she would rather not have had. Today the chapel has gone. In its place is the Working Men's Club and you could drive past it every day and not know what lies there.

There is, however, a postscript. An article appeared in the press in 1866. Thomas Williams - or Screens - was by then living in lodgings within 100 yards of her grave. He was:

> 'looked upon as one half broken hearted. He was strange in manner in the works and appeared on the verge of insanity.'

He was said to have emigrated to Australia.

Yet the story doesn't even end there.

There is a statement given by a Mr. Richard Packer from Treforest in 1902, which is held by the South Wales Police. In it he talks about the time he spent in Australia. One afternoon he met a man who was behaving strangely. He was 'picking up stones and then throwing them at the doors of the houses as he walked along.' He asked Packer if he was Welsh, for he recognised his flannel shirt. Then the man told him:

> "I come from the Rhondda valley. Did you hear of the murder of Jane Lewis of Tyntila? It was I that killed her".

Throwing stones at houses in Australia? Perhaps guilt did indeed have 'its proper reward.' ✒

THE HEADSTONE OF AENON CHAPEL ITSELF LIES IN THE GRASS ALONG WITH JANE'S GRAVE AND THOSE OF OTHER MEMBERS OF HER FAMILY

Joseph Butler
SHOT

The village of Llanafan lies a short way off the B4340 between Aberystwyth and Pontrhydfendigaid. St Afan's Church is in the centre of the village.

Go into the churchyard through the lych gate and there to the left, against the perimeter wall, you will find him, looking up at the stained glass window and the church bells. The writing is starting to fade but you can still make it out if you look closely.

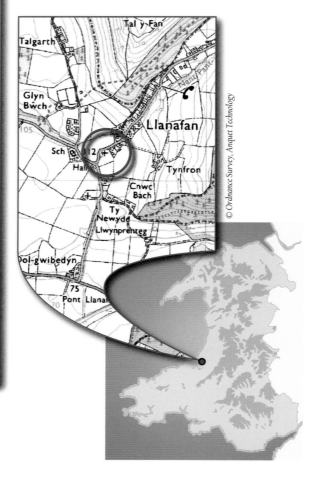

© Ordnance Survey, Anquet Technology

Murder seems to have followed St Afan around. As we have seen, he shares his resting place in Llanafan Fawr with the murder victim John Price from 1826 (see Page 50). This time we must visit the church of St Afan in Llanafan, about 7 miles south east of Aberystwyth, which shelters against its wall the grave of Joseph Butler.

Poor Joseph was murdered too.

Sacred to the memory of Joseph Butler,
GameKeeper Crosswood,
Who was shot by a poacher,
28 November 1868, Aged 29 years.

He shares his grave with another gamekeeper, James Martin, who died in December 1882 aged 32. They are now watched over by grazing sheep and everything seems peaceful and untroubled here in the Ystwyth valley. It is such a peaceful setting that it is hard to equate such surroundings with violence, pain and suffering. But theirs was a risky profession in those days, with danger in the night, guns, hostility, unpopularity. Being a gamekeeper was never a job for the faint hearted. There were those who

JOSEPH BUTLER

1868

LLANAFAN

MORE DANGEROUS
THAN BEING A
SOLDIER

said that it was more dangerous than being a soldier. Look what it did to Joseph Butler. It killed him. No preparation, no warning, just a single shot in the night.

William Richards of Cefn Coch and two brothers, Morgan and Henry Jones went out to poach in Dolfor Wood, owned by Lord Lisburne. It was part of the large Trawsgoed estate that employed five gamekeepers to preserve the valuable stocks it held. There was profit to be made here and to assist in realising such profits, Wil and Morgan carried guns whilst the 14 year old Henry had a stick.

That night there was no sign of gamekeepers anywhere. It was easy work to lay some snares. But Wil foolishly shot a couple of hares and in the cold clear night the sound carried far away and the gamekeepers came at speed from a neighbouring wood. The poachers heard them and fled but were outflanked in the open fields.

Morgan was grabbed by a gamekeeper called James Morgan, who shouted excitedly to his colleagues to join him. Morgan Jones

St. Afan's Church in Llanafan

shouted and screamed but the unarmed gamekeeper was not going to let him go. So Wil pointed his gun at him. The gamekeeper pleaded with him in Welsh not to shoot whilst maintaining his grip on the frightened poacher. The other gamekeepers rushed to them. Wil turned and fired straight into the chest of Joseph Butler who was about 12 inches away from the muzzle of his gun. A shot fired cannot be recalled. A sudden and almost random act, born of fear and stupidity and Joseph lay dead on the ground.

The gamekeepers were in shock and stared at poor Joseph, though they still held on to Morgan. Wil and Henry were shocked too, but fled the scene at speed. In this unthinking moment Wil's life was defined for him.

Everyone knew that Wil had done it, of this there could be no doubt and so Wil Cefn Coch became a wanted man. But he also became a folk hero because they never caught him. One of the biggest manhunts in the history of West Wales was made futile because he was sheltered and protected and ultimately spirited away. He may indeed have been a drunk with a violent temper and he certainly killed an innocent man. Yet these things counted for nothing. No one wanted to see him hang.

To understand why a murderer should become a hero, it is necessary to understand the enormous significance that poaching had in a rural community like Cardiganshire.

Poaching encapsulated the enduring class struggle. Men - and boys - living in abject rural poverty would be severely punished for trying to provide for their families from the land on which they lived and worked.

MORGAN JONES SHOUTED AND SCREAMED BUT THE UNARMED GAMEKEEPER WAS NOT GOING TO LET HIM GO

They might have provided the labour, but the land was not theirs. It was parcelled off and confined. It seemed to exist to support others, even to support animals, but not to support them. The only solution for a hungry family was to do that which others described as theft. Folk tradition is littered with stories and songs about poachers. Look at this verse from the song, "The Rufford Park Poacher."

> A buck or doe, believe it so,
> A pheasant or a hare,
> Were set on earth for everyone
> Quite equally to share.

This was the myth, but if only it were so simple.

Landowners had little sympathy at all. They believed that there was no connection between poverty and poaching. It wasn't about survival, it was about profit. Just as we tend to regard the proceeds of begging on the streets of London as an integral part of the drugs trade, they thought the profits from poaching were spent in the pubs. Traditionally poachers made plans in the pubs and thus spent their money there. Poaching wasn't about survival at all. It was theft, pure and simple. Indeed the big estates were creating wealth; they had nothing to do with poverty.

What they saw was that London-based gangs maintained a huge controlling influence over the poaching economy. These gangs grew steadily in size from about 1830 and their representatives would make contact with actual poachers in rural areas. The arrival of the train to the remotest parts of Wales made it much simpler to fulfil orders for the London market.

It was a fine example of supply and demand in perfect harmony. Quite simply there were more animals to be poached. Estate owners were building up their game and fish stocks for angling and shooting groups who were prepared to pay well for easy sport. A practice still much in evidence today. But they were not prepared to see their precious stock staring sightlessly from a cart in a London market.

The law had long been mobilised against the poacher. There was the Night Poaching Act 1828 and the Game Act of 1831. Anyone suspected of carrying poaching implements could be stopped and searched by the police under The Poaching Prevention Act of 1862. In fact, poachers were treated more harshly than any other people accused of other types of theft. Imprisonment and transportation were common, the latter being viewed with true horror by country people who would have rarely travelled any further than the nearest market.

The myth of the noble poacher, however, survived. They were resourceful and clever individuals who were prepared to take on the establishment. Yet sometimes, the representatives of that privileged world they confronted in the night were people much like themselves.

Gamekeepers.

Don't forget that expression, "Poacher turned gamekeeper". They were the same people, but in direct opposition. So gamekeepers were as unpopular as only a class-traitor can be. The famous folk song "The Lincolnshire Poacher" makes this point.

> As me and my companions was setting
> out a snare
> 'Twas then we spied the gamekeeper,
> for him we didn't care

Their vulnerabilities never troubled

THE AGE-OLD CERTAINTIES OF DEFERENCE TO THE SQUIRE NO LONGER SEEMED RELEVANT

anyone. Yet they had to confront men with guns in the woods or fields in the middle of the night - with sometimes fatal consequences as we can see.

So two extremes of the rural community were set against each other, with the gamekeeper in the middle. The community they came from asked one question: why should rich people make themselves richer

WHY SHOULD RICH PEOPLE MAKE THEMSELVES RICHER FROM THE LAND, WHILST THE POOR WHO WORKED ON IT REMAINED HUNGRY?

from the land, whilst the poor who worked on it remained hungry? So poachers were thought of as heroes. They were rescued from the hands of keepers and police and hidden and supported. This goes some way towards explaining why the community sheltered a murderer like Wil Cefn Coch.

There were other forces at work too; the community was changing. The Vaughan family who owned the estate were the largest landowners in Cardiganshire and enjoyed the hereditary title of the Earls of Lisburne. But the 28 November

was a significant date for them; it was a parliamentary election in Cardiganshire and Edward Vaughan, as the Tory candidate, was expected to win - except he didn't. The electoral franchise had been extended and a liberal tradition was suddenly established. The age-old certainties of deference to the squire no longer seemed relevant. Vaughan's valet had been beaten up in Aberystwyth on Election Day. The community seemed to be turning against him. The death of his gamekeeper was suddenly a symbol of this loss of control. He offered the sizeable reward of £100 for information leading to the arrest of Wil Cefn Coch. It was a huge amount of money, capable of transforming the finances of any impoverished family in the community he used to control. But now he could no longer buy either their support or their information. It just wasn't enough to prompt a betrayal.

Morgan Jones of course was in custody and his terrified brother Henry gave himself up almost immediately. Wil, however, seemed to have disappeared. The whole of West Wales was flooded with posters offering the reward. On the posters he is described as "a slight figure, long thin legs, with stooping gait" and his most distinguishing feature is the fact that he 'has been operated upon for a bruise in the testicle' which obviously made him stand out like a sore thumb.

But people were ready to shelter him. It is said that on one occasion he hid from the police under the counterpane of a newly-delivered mother. It is claimed that he hid beneath the waterwheel of a local mill. He hid in chapels, chimneys and copses. But it couldn't go on forever. Obvious escape routes like Aberaeron harbour were closely guarded and the winter cold would eventually break the resolve of someone in the community. His friends finally got him out of the immediate area by hiding him in a manure cart and Wil made his way to Liverpool. Here he boarded a ship to America disguised as a woman in the spring of 1869. The search for the murderer of Joseph Butler was eventually abandoned.

Morgan Jones was brought to trial in March 1869 but he could hardly be charged as an accessory to murder since he was being held securely by James Morgan when the shot was fired. He was sentenced to one year's hard labour for poaching. His brother was never brought to trial due to a lack of conclusive evidence.

So then, what of William Richards, murderer? He settled into the Welsh community in Oak Hill, Ohio in the name of Evan Morgan. He worked casually as a farm labourer. He established a reputation as a brooding unpredictable figure, prone to drunkenness and aggression. There were scenes and incidents. He was ridiculed for his poor grasp of English. He was a dangerous outsider. However, he was, in part, rescued through marriage. His beloved, Elizabeth Morgan, who worked for two years in London to pay for her passage, emigrated with two brothers to Ohio in 1872 to join him. They married and lived under the name of Evans, for Wil was always haunted by his past. They say he always slept with a loaded revolver beneath his pillow, but then perhaps everyone did in Ohio in those days. They ran their own farm and Wil operated as a coal merchant. They had no children. Wil died in 1921, after spending over fifty years in exile. Elizabeth lived on until 1937.

And all this time in the quiet churchyard in Llanafan the rain continued to fall on the grave of Joseph Butler. ᕗ

Sarah Jacob
STARVED

1869
LLANFIHANGEL
AR ARTH

Take the B4336 out of Llandysul, driving up the hill out of town to the east. At the crossroads in Llanfihangel ar Arth turn left and go down the hill. You will come to a sharp right hand bend in the road. There you will see the pub The Eagle, where the inquest was held, on the right. The churchyard of St Michael's is immediately in front of you.

Enter and on the left, a short way along the main path, you will find the doctor. The vicar is to the right of the main door of the church itself. To find poor Sarah and her family, you must stay on the left hand side of the church and descend through the grass, right down to the very bottom corner.

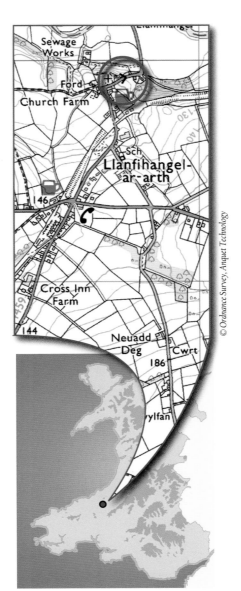

© Ordnance Survey, Anquet Technology

There is a grave down in the far corner of the cemetery of St. Michael's Church in Llanfihangel ar Arth. We look at it and consider the tragedy it represents with incredulity. How could anyone let this happen? For this is the grave of a 12 year old girl, allowed to starve herself to death.

This is the grave of Sarah Jacob, the Welsh Fasting Girl.

Technically this wasn't a murder. In court the verdict was manslaughter. The other possible verdict would have been suicide. But in every other sense it was a murder, and a cruel and heartless one.

For a short while this little village near Llandysul became the centre of national attention and it was all because of the vicar, Reverend Jones.

Sarah Jacob was born on 12 May 1857 at Lletherneuadd. Her parents Evan and Hannah lived a hard life on the farm, the sort of life that had not changed for centuries. Isolated, self-sufficient, unsophisticated. Sarah, their third child, was bright and lively.

On 15 February 1867 she fell seriously ill. What she had isn't quite clear and certainly went way beyond the experience of Henry Harries Davies, the doctor from Llandysul, who was eventually called. 'Catalepsy,' he said. He didn't really know. She was suffering from convulsions and spasms and was clearly not expected to live. It is said that she was unconscious for a month, during which time she had little food. She was in:

> 'some kind of permanent fit, living on her back, with rigidity of all muscles.'

IT IS SAID THAT SHE WAS UNCONSCIOUS FOR A MONTH, DURING WHICH TIME SHE HAD LITTLE FOOD

Our best guess today would be that she had viral encephalitis. It should be noted that survivors of the illness are often left with brain damage.

But Sarah didn't die and she showed some signs of recovery. She would eat a little rice or oatmeal and milk but this was:

> 'cast up again immediately and blood and froth with it.'

The amount she would eat dwindled until it was nothing more than a small piece of apple. Her parents later declared that they stopped feeding her altogether on 10 October 1867. Sarah had convinced them that the very act of swallowing would kill her. Whenever food was either mentioned or offered, Sarah would appear to have a fit. So they stopped feeding her and she appeared to improve. Soon the local people were visiting the farm to see the girl with the wonderful fasting powers.

She would lie in bed to receive visitors, with the family Bible and surrounded by religious books. Soon she was dressed in elaborate fantasy clothes - a shawl and ribbons, wild flowers, a wreath in her hair.

Her mother said "She had no other pleasure." Dressed like a little doll, hiding from the real world. Frightened by her close encounter with death, but pleased by the attention she was receiving. Small gifts or money were left by visitors and her fame spread; a wonderful little girl who lived and improved without food.

All nonsense of course. Her sister may have been slipping her food or she might have risen in the night and helped herself. Although the family shared one bedroom, her parent's bed was curtained. Just a little game, a bit of attention for a child who had so narrowly escaped death. The family were so relieved at her survival that they indulged her

Andrzej Puchta

SOON SHE WAS DRESSED IN ELABORATE FANTASY
CLOTHES – A SHAWL AND RIBBONS, WILD FLOWERS,
A WREATH IN HER HAIR

UNDER SUCH CLOSE AND PROFESSIONAL SCRUTINY SOMETHING HAD TO GIVE.

THEY LET HER DIE TO PROVE A POINT

Sarah's gravestone

deception, fulfilled her need for attention and confirmed their own uncomplicated beliefs.

The vicar, Reverend Evan Jones, was called for and he claimed later that he:

'remonstrated with them and dwelt upon the apparent impossibility of the thing...I then dwelt upon the sinfulness of continuing the fraud.'

HER PARENTS LATER DECLARED THAT THEY STOPPED FEEDING HER ALTOGETHER ON 10 OCTOBER 1867

But as Sarah appeared to thrive over that winter, he eventually changed his tune. He had his own reasons for wanting it to be true. He was emotionally very vulnerable. His wife died from typhoid in 1868, leaving him with two daughters. He needed something to believe in. So he believed Sarah. She was a miracle. He wrote to the press.

'She is...a wonderful little girl'

He poured scorn upon the medical profession who said that her survival was impossible and suggested that her case be put to the test.

'Mr. Evan Jacob would readily admit into his house any respectable person who might be anxious to watch and to see for himself.'

The consequences of an Anglican vicar declaring a miracle never occurred to him. The doctor, too, was ready to declare her a phenomenon, despite sceptical comments in the medical press.

A public meeting was organised and a team of watchers appointed who would sit with Sarah and confirm that there was no subterfuge. The watch, involving a team of local men, and organised by Dr. Davies and Reverend Jones, began on 22 March 1869 for a fortnight and was a shambles. The watchers slept or were drunk and Sarah found them easy to outwit. To her it must have been a little game. At the end of the watching, the conclusion was that she was indeed surviving without food. The doctor and the vicar had been vindicated. She was a miracle.

Despite the fact that she continually wet the bed.

Of course the notoriety of the case became ever greater. Her story appeared in the national press, Dickens wrote an article about 'Fasting Girls', people flocked to West Wales to see her. At the nearest train station in Pencader, visitors were met by boys with signs reading 'The Fasting Girl,' 'This is the shortest way to Lletherneuadd.' Sarah Jacob had become a show girl and an industry.

THAT SARAH HAD BEEN INVOLVED IN A DECEPTION THERE CAN BE NO DOUBT

She became a curiosity, a symbol of a vanishing way of life. The people who travelled from England to see her in her Welsh isolation came on the trains that would, in such a short time, connect rural West Wales to the rest of the world forever. Her community was looked down upon for its rural simplicity. It was a backward place, with strange and absurd beliefs, speaking in a foreign language. The people were in need of civilisation, not superstition. The claims made for her were a consequence of 'the credulity of Welsh persons.' Reverend Jones was held up to ridicule, whilst he in his turn described medicine as 'the most uncertain and most immature of sciences.' Never forget that doctors had been unable to save the life of his wife.

The medical establishment responded angrily. This was a real conflict between science and superstition, between educated urban English professionals and, in their eyes, Welsh-speaking peasants. Doctors were sent from London and they viewed the scene in the farm with less reverence and more suspicion. A Scottish physician on holiday in Cardigan, Dr. Robert Fowler, went to see her and carried out an examination.

> 'The child was lying on a bed decorated as a bride. Her face was plump and her cheeks and lips of a beautiful rosy colour...There was that restless movement and frequent looking out at the corners of the eyes so characteristic of simulative disease.'

He was not prepared to be distracted from his examination of her by Sarah's alleged fits which had so often prevented others from completing theirs. He heard sounds of her digestive tract at work. He noted the absence of bedsores. His conclusions were clear.

> 'The whole case is in fact one of simulated hysteria, in a young girl having the propensity to deceive very strongly developed.'

Her supporters could not accept such a conclusion. To do so would mean that someone was lying, that they had been deceived by a seemingly innocent little girl. Dr. Davies? Reverend Jones? Not possible.

Later in his career Fowler would be instrumental in identifying the condition of anorexia nervosa. Here he unwittingly set in motion the events that would lead to Sarah's death. She should be treated in more controlled conditions he said, in a hospital. But since her parents would not let her be taken away, a new watch was agreed, this time supervised by doctors and carried out by London nurses from Guy's hospital. Sarah's fate was sealed.

An official world came from nowhere and took over. To confront a simple family with scientific proof. To allow her to die.

That Sarah had been involved in a deception there can be no doubt. Perhaps others too - maybe her sister Margaret, who was frequently put into Sarah's bed to keep her warm and she was forever by the bedside. But her parents never questioned her. They had no doubts. They believed Sarah. Her convulsions or fits they regarded as a divine visitation.

Sarah had discovered through illness that she could manipulate her parents. They were busy, hardworking people, yet she could force them to give her time and attention. Only Dadda was allowed to change her bedding, no matter how busy he was. She enjoyed it, sitting in bed decorated and adorned.

But suddenly she found herself completely out of her depth. All that control was taken away from her because others had a different agenda, and one that lay outside her experience. Suddenly she was backed into a corner from which there was no escape. She obviously felt she had to maintain her deception, but under such close and professional scrutiny something had to give and they let her die to prove a point.

Different times perhaps, with different beliefs, but nothing can excuse such bone-headed stupidity.

The watching began on 9 December 1869 and this time there was no escape. Those around her seemed to have lost sight of her identity as a person. She was now part of a scientific assault on superstition.

The nurses could not be fooled and Sarah went into a steady and inexorable decline. No one did anything to stop it. She stubbornly refused to give in and her parents clung to their belief in her. This had happened before. Her decline had nothing to do with a lack of food, because of course they hadn't been feeding her, so why should it? They believed that God provided for Sarah so there was no need for the nurses to be withdrawn or for the watch to end.

In the middle of the afternoon on 17 December 1869 Sarah Jacob died, 'starved to death in the middle of the nineteenth century and in one of the most Christian and civilised countries of the world.' She died in the presence of doctors and nurses and her family, any of whom could have saved her.

The inquest discovered marks on her toe where she had tried to secretly remove the stopper of her hot water bottle. Her armpit had a well-worn depression where she had stored things.

People were horrified. How could anyone let this happen? The coroner held that the responsibility rested with the father, 'who had knowingly and designedly failed to cause his child to take food.' How could anyone have believed the claims were true? The story of the Fasting Girl was a 'hideous mass of nonsense.'

To us, the whole sorry mess seems ridiculous, and it was. There can never have been any justification for what they did. Someone needed to take responsibility, but not one of the professionals did.

Sarah was part of a struggle between science and faith and only afterwards did there seem to be any recognition that there was a child involved. The Medical Press and Circular was especially pompous:

'This case has concluded as every rational man must have foreseen. The watching was carried out with commendable zeal and yet kindness to the sufferer.'

The rest of the press however were outraged. The Daily News observed:

'Fraud and deception ought to be detected and exposed but is not the penalty of death too heavy a one for this childish imposture?'

The Times said:

'Her end is as piteous as it is extraordinary. It is the death of a martyr without a martyr's objects.'

The Pall Mall Gazette said:

'The death of the Welsh Fasting Girl ought to make some of us feel very much ashamed of ourselves. What business was it of ours whether she took food or not? We have covered ourselves with confusion and disgrace.'

Someone had to pay the price.

Not the doctors. The parents.

An inquest was held in the Eagle Inn opposite the church. The Coroner recommended a charge of manslaughter and Evan and Hannah were arrested.

The doctor's grave

SARAH DIED IN THE PRESENCE OF DOCTORS AND NURSES AND HER FAMILY, ANY OF WHOM COULD HAVE SAVED HER

SOMEONE HAD TO
PAY THE PRICE.

NOT THE DOCTORS.
THE PARENTS

The Eagle Pub, where Sarah's inquest was held

Charges against anyone else were dropped.

They appeared in Carmarthen in July 1870. The charges were read to them in Welsh, but they were tried in English. They were found guilty. The judge said,

> 'The life of that child has been lost in that wicked experiment which you tried. Therefore the sentence that I shall inflict on you, Evan Jacob, is that you be imprisoned and kept at hard labour for twelve calendar months; and that upon you, Hannah Jacob, will be more lenient and that you be imprisoned and kept to hard labour for the period of six calendar months.'

Hannah, confused and still grieving, was put to sewing mailbags. Evan was sent to the treadmill in Swansea.

So punishment came - but not to the professionals who sat and watched her. The doctors were not prosecuted. The vicar never appeared in court. Only the parents who believed her.

You can find them all in St. Michael's Churchyard. The Reverend Evan Jones died in 1904. He is by the porch. 'Peace Perfect Peace' is the inscription on his tomb. By the path you can see Henry Harries Davies, the doctor. He died in 1913 and is also remembered on a plaque inside the well-kept church. 'Glorious is the fruit of good labours,' we are told. Apparently he 'practised the Divine Art of Healing.'

In the bottom corner of the graveyard, down where the grass is long and wet and a hedge reaches out to obscure it, you will find the Jacob grave. Overgrown. Neglected. Untidy. Evan died in 1895 and Hannah in 1907. They are remembered with Sarah and their other children. The faint inscription reads:

> 'Dy ewyllys di a weler.'
> 'Behold! Thy will.'

Sarah's story is a significant record, a documented example of an eating disorder. An important case, though of course Sarah Jacob was not the first; there had been others before, and she wouldn't be the last.

Today we call them eating disorders and ascribe a psychological cause, but most importantly, we do our very best to ensure that we don't let our children die. ✦

Based upon an article that first appeared in Welsh Country magazine in Jan/Feb and Mar/Apr 2006

1876

John Johnes
MURDERED CAIO

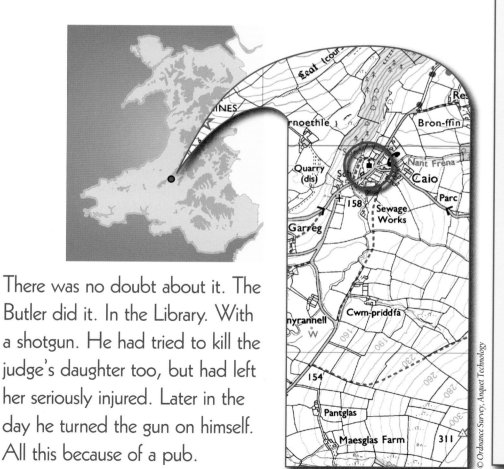

© Ordnance Survey, Anquet Technology

There was no doubt about it. The Butler did it. In the Library. With a shotgun. He had tried to kill the judge's daughter too, but had left her seriously injured. Later in the day he turned the gun on himself. All this because of a pub.

You will find the grave very easily. Travel along the A482 between Llanwrda, in Carmarthenshire, and Lampeter. This road takes you through the village of Pumpsaint and past the Dolaucothi Arms that played an important part in the dispute.

Take the turning from this road that is signposted Caio. Drive to the centre of the village. You can park on the left quite easily before you reach the church.

Enter the churchyard through the gate. You will find a reference here to another member of the Johnes family, Sir James Hills-Johnes who was awarded the Victoria Cross for gallantry at the siege of Dehli in 1857. Then look at the rear of the church to the right where you will find the railings that mark off the Johnes vault.

THERE WAS
NO DOUBT
ABOUT IT.

THE
BUTLER
DID IT.

IN THE
LIBRARY.

WITH A
SHOTGUN.

The Sexton's Inn in Caio, where Henry Tremble was once the tenant

TREMBLE'S REVENGE WAS CAREFULLY FOCUSED. HE WAS
NOT A DERANGED MASS MURDERER. IN HIS OWN MIND
HE HAD GOOD REASONS FOR WHAT HE DID

The Western Mail, Monday August 21st, 1876:

'Mr. John Johnes, formerly judge of the county court for the counties of Carmarthen, Cardigan and Pembroke, chairman of the Carmarthenshire quarter sessions, and recorder of the borough of Carmarthenshire, was assassinated on Saturday at his seat, Dolaucothy, near Llandilo, by his butler, Henry Tremble.'

Johnes had retired in 1870 after a distinguished career and lived in Dolaucothi Mansion with his two daughters Bertha Johnes and Charlotte Cookman, a widow. It was a comfortable and quiet life, their needs attended to by loyal servants. One of these was Henry Tremble. Henry had originally been the valet to Captain Cookman and, when Charlotte returned home to Wales on her husband's death, he had come with her. What his origins were isn't really clear but he regarded himself as an Irishman.

In Dolaucothi he worked his way up through the strictly delineated levels of life in service. He started as a stable boy, and then became coachman. Eventually he became butler and confidential servant to the judge. Significantly, he also acted as part-time gamekeeper. This gave him access to the guns in the house.

He was married to Martha, the daughter of a local farmer and they had 6 children. However it was not a happy marriage, for Henry developed deep and apparently unfounded suspicions about his wife's fidelity. It changed him. Once pleasant and accommodating, he became surly and uncooperative. Johnes considered dismissing

THE HOUSEMAID FOUND JOHNES SLUMPED AT HIS DESK, CONSCIOUS, BUT WITH A LARGE PART OF HIS INTESTINES EXPOSED

him on a number of occasions, but was prevented from doing so by Charlotte, who remembered always that Tremble had been her husband's favourite servant. She said that 'he had never received anything but the utmost kindness from us.' Such misplaced loyalty would lead to tragedy.

There were other problems for Henry too. At one point, as well as his work in service, he had also been tenant of the public house, The Sexton's Inn, in Caio. The venture had failed and the family had moved to Myrtle

Cottage. Obviously Henry Tremble couldn't run a pub; the conclusion was inescapable.

But he thought he could.

CHARLOTTE'S JOURNAL IS A CHILLING AND DETAILED ACCOUNT OF THIS VIOLENT AND HORRIBLE EXPLOSION OF MADNESS

So, in July 1876, Henry applied to the judge for the vacant lease of the Dolaucothi Arms in Pumpsaint. Johnes turned him down. Arguments ensued, and the relationship between gentleman and butler broke down completely. Tremble was dismissed.

It isn't hard to imagine his state of mind. Treated badly by a family to whom he had devoted his life, his understandable ambition to improve the lifestyle of his family dismissed out of hand. Some crony put in his rightful place as host of a well-appointed hostelry. Something inside him snapped; he wanted revenge.

As was his custom, Johnes took his breakfast in the Library at 10.00 am on Saturday 19 August. He had had a pleasant few moments discussing with his daughter the differences between an aneroid and a barometer. Then, as breakfast was served Henry Tremble entered. He was carrying a shotgun. There may have been words, a discussion, pleas for re-instatement; we shall never know. What we do know however is that Tremble shot him once, in the abdomen. The housemaid ran in to find Johnes slumped at his desk, conscious, but with a large part of his intestines exposed. "I have been shot by Tremble," he groaned. "I am dying. Henry Tremble shot me. See that he is taken." He died two hours later. His last words were, "God bless my children and I know He will bless them."

Charlotte was in the kitchen with the cook, Margaret Davies, talking about raspberry vinegar. On hearing the shot she went to the library, but met Tremble in the corridor. He forced her back into the kitchen, with the gun pointing at her chest. Margaret stepped between them and refused to move. So he pushed the gun under her arm and fired. He hit Charlotte in the thigh and the groin. Much of the detail that we have comes from Charlotte's Journal. It is a chilling and detailed account of this violent and horrible explosion of madness. She writes:

'He took deliberate aim and said, "Take that for your persecution of me."... I saw the fire come out of the muzzle of the gun. I turned

SOMETHING INSIDE TREMBLE SNAPPED AND HE WANTED REVENGE

suddenly round and the whole charge entered my back and down my thigh, I fell on my face towards the scullery door.'

The maid Anna Dixon came in to find the two women slumped on the floor, one bleeding profusely, with Tremble calmly reloading his gun. "I do not care for God, Man or the Devil." He pointed at Charlotte. "If I thought she were not dead I would beat out her brains with the butt of the gun." Anna backed out of the kitchen and ran away. This saved her life. Indeed, Charlotte reports that he had told Anna the previous night that she would not be living in the house too long after his departure. At the time of course these words signified little. For his part he went outside to the kennels and shot all the judge's dogs. Tremble called two other servants to him, Benny the gardener and Thomas the Waggoner, but observing what he had done they felt it better to stay where they were.

Then he set off for Caio. He was looking for John Davies, the landlord of the Caio Inn - because Johnes had selected him as tenant of the Dolaucothi Arms. He couldn't find him though.

Tremble's revenge was carefully focused. He was not a deranged mass murderer. In his own mind he had good reasons for what he did. On his way to Caio he met a policeman, Constable Davies. He stuck his gun in the constable's chest and told him that if he didn't turn away he would shoot him. Davies did as Tremble said and ran off to raise the alarm. Tremble did nothing to stop him. He then met a man called William Morgan. He told him that he had shot Johnes and that, since he had a horse, it was Morgan's duty to ride to Llandovery to fetch a surgeon. Tremble refused to hand over the gun because he was looking for Davies and because he needed it to defend himself from the police. Morgan was not sure whether all this was true but agreed to ride to Llandovery. When he said that he would be back in the afternoon, Tremble replied, "By then I will be dead."

TREMBLE'S GRAVE WAS OPENED AND THE
COFFIN TAKEN IN THE MIDDLE OF THE NIGHT
TO LLANDULAIS FOR REBURIAL

Whilst Morgan was on his mission, the police in Llandeilo heard the news. Constables, under the command of Superintendent Durnford, were dispatched for Caio, setting up roadblocks as they went. But there was no need. Tremble was holed up at home in Myrtle Cottage.

When William Morgan returned from Llandovery on that Saturday afternoon, he saw that the police had surrounded the cottage. Tremble was at an upstairs window, waving guns about. He shouted to Morgan.

> "Keep those men away for I do not want to take innocent lives. If they attempt to interfere with me I'll shoot them like dogs."

Morgan tried to persuade him to give himself up but Tremble laughed off the suggestion. It had been his intention to kill Johnes and Mrs Cookman and he would spare his family the shame of a hanging by committing suicide.

He had already written his will a couple of weeks earlier. It ends with a PS: 'There will be about £8 in my pocket.' Everything was carefully planned.

There was a shot and the police broke into the cottage. Tremble had ripped open his shirt and shot himself in the chest with his shotgun. He died 15 minutes later.

Left: The Dolaucothi Arms in Pumpsaint

In his own mind Tremble had a perfect justification. Whatever other storms and angers flooded his mind, one thing he could grasp with absolute conviction: everything that was going wrong in his life was the responsibility of the Johnes family. He had been wronged and he believed in his right to revenge. His killing wasn't indiscriminate; he had no desire to harm any innocent person. It was planned vengeance. His only regret seemed to be that Charlotte had survived.

IN HIS OWN MIND TREMBLE HAD A PERFECT JUSTIFICATION

For her part she says:

> 'Take note that the murderer was perfectly sane and not drunk or an habitual drunkard - the sole reason for the diabolical crimes was that Papa (for many just and cogent reasons) refused to let him the Dolau Cothy Arms Inn at Pumpsaint. Whereupon he gave warning and from that moment must have meditated the hideous crime of murder.'

John Johnes was buried alongside his wife and mother in the family vault in the churchyard in Caio on 26 August 1876. The church was draped in black and the path to

THE WARDENS BURIED HIM AGAIN IN CAIO, BUT THIS TIME THEY DIDN'T TELL ANYONE WHERE IN THE GRAVEYARD THEY PUT HIM

the vault decorated with flowers. It was the same churchyard where Henry Tremble had been buried a few days earlier, at eleven in the evening on 21 August.

Some people found the idea that Tremble and Johnes were buried in the same churchyard rather difficult to accept. So Tremble's grave was opened and the coffin taken in the middle of the night to Llandulais in Powys for reburial.

The gravedigger was told that it was the body of a foreigner. But suspicions were aroused when he examined the burial certificate and discovered that it was a blank piece of paper. When, after about three months, they worked out who the foreigner

was, the good people of Llandulais wouldn't have him. He was a murderer and he wasn't belonging.

So they dug up Henry and took him back to Caio where they intended to bury him. But they got lost on the way and didn't arrive until dawn. They had no time for digging so Tremble's coffin was left on the churchyard path, with a note kept in place on the coffin by four stones, explaining their actions. It is said that on the way home they disposed of the straw they had used to cover the coffin by throwing it into a ditch near Aberbowlan. For years afterwards the children of the area were frightened by stories of the 'bwgan' that lived in that ditch.

The wardens buried him again in Caio, but this time they didn't tell anyone where in the graveyard they put him. You will find the Johnes vault at the northeast end of the church. Today it is rather neglected and the railings around it rusted and forlorn. But of Henry Tremble there is no trace.

He is still there.

Somewhere.

Probably. &

Based upon an article that first appeared in Welsh Country magazine in May/Jun 2006

THE MURDERER WAS PERFECTLY SANE AND THE SOLE
REASON FOR HIS CRIMES WAS THAT HE WAS REFUSED
TENANCY OF THE DOLAUCOTHY ARMS INN

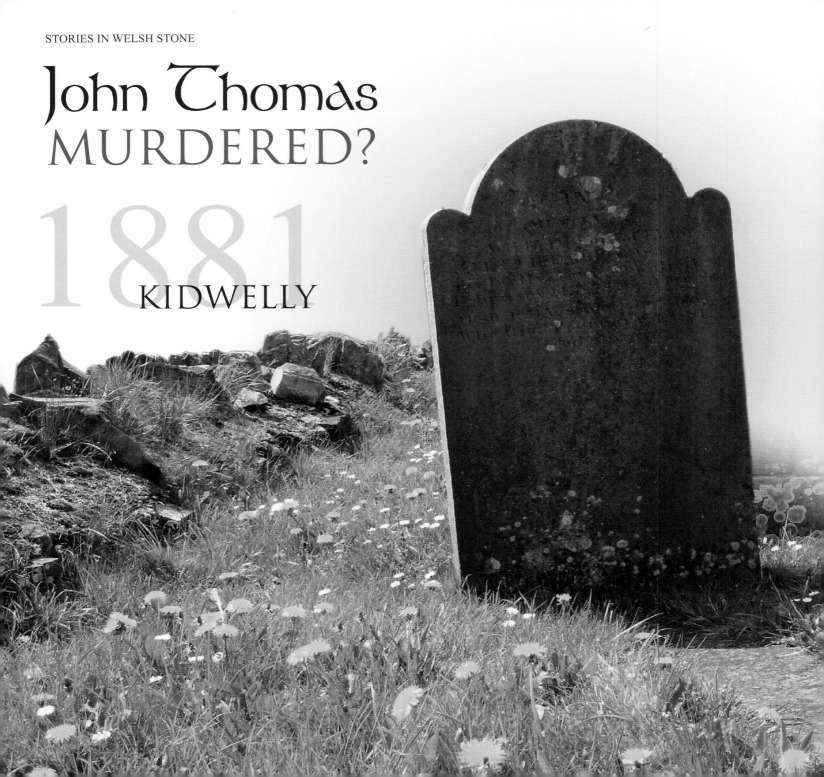

STORIES IN WELSH STONE

John Thomas
MURDERED?

1881
KIDWELLY

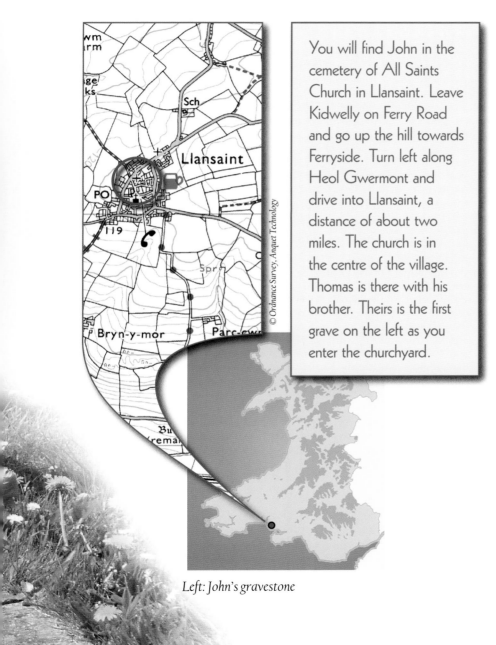

You will find John in the cemetery of All Saints Church in Llansaint. Leave Kidwelly on Ferry Road and go up the hill towards Ferryside. Turn left along Heol Gwermont and drive into Llansaint, a distance of about two miles. The church is in the centre of the village. Thomas is there with his brother. Theirs is the first grave on the left as you enter the churchyard.

© Ordnance Survey, Anquet Technology

Left: John's gravestone

So did John Thomas die in a horrible childhood accident? Or did he meet his end at the hands of a cold-eyed killer? Or two killers? Or perhaps even three?

Judge for yourself.

Where John Thomas now lies is a quiet and attractive place and when the light catches the stone at the right angle you can read the inscription clearly:

William, son of Evan and Letitia Thomas of Kidwelly Town, who died February 11 1878 aged 14.
Also John, son of the above, who died February 4 1881, aged 11.

Poor John. Killed on an errand in Kidwelly.

Poor Evan and Letitia. February must have been such a grim month for them. Two sons. One grave. Families could be so fragile in those days.

Evan was a shoemaker who lived with his family in Tin Mill Row. The family were honest, though poor, known for their hard work and thrift. On Wednesday 2 February

131

1881 Evan sent his 11 year old son John to deliver a pair of shoes to Mr. Anthony of Muddlescombe Farm. It was a distance of about a mile. On arrival John was paid a half sovereign and told to return with the necessary one shilling change. He was given some lunch and he left at 2.30 pm.

His journey took him past the home of David Mazey and his family. Mazey was an Irishman who worked at the tinplate works. He was married to Jane, his second wife, and they had two boys, David and Benjamin. Their house was a wreck. It was called Stockwell and was old and decaying. The garden was overgrown and the windows lacked glass, being covered by having old clothes draped over them. The family were not well liked. Jane was described as aggressive and vindictive. The two boys, aged 10 and 12 were often beaten viciously by their mother and had developed a reputation of their own.

In 1880 they had been involved in a rather suspicious incident. In August they had been playing with a boy called Fisher down by the river. Half an hour later they returned home carrying his clothes, saying he had drowned. At the inquest young David Mazey said they had walked into the water together and that Fisher had sunk out of sight. There were no other witnesses. Tongues wagged. These boys were dangerous, unruly, and, whilst nothing could be proved, perhaps liars too. Best to stay away. But boys don't listen, do they?

It was on his way home to get the change that John Thomas disappeared. Soon his anxious parents were searching for him. Was he playing? Hiding? Lost? And when was the last time anyone had seen John? Well a neighbour had seen him going into the Mazey house. In the evening Evan and Letitia called on the Mazeys, but Jane denied that John had been there. She refused to ask her boys about it, saying that they were asleep. I am sure Evan and Letitia didn't sleep much.

A full scale search was organised the next day, but of John there was no sign. Then that night Jane Mazey turned up at the Thomas house, expressing concern and offering support. Suddenly, she revealed that John had been playing in front of her fire with a half sovereign and that from somewhere or other he'd given one of her boys a half crown. The Thomas' were not to worry. She would pay them back. Letitia said that she would rather have her son than the money. But at least they had a lead.

On the Friday the police went straight to the Mazey house. They found the body, partially covered by weeds in a ditch in the overgrown garden. John's skull was completely split open. His brains they found in a neighbouring garden. There was an inescapable conclusion. The police immediately arrested the two boys and their mother and charged them with wilful murder.

Kidwelly was in uproar. The brutality of the crime and the reputation of the Mazeys was enough. They were obviously guilty.

People gathered at Stockwell to view the place where the body was discovered. They would also have seen the simple swing hanging from an apple tree in the middle of the garden. It was merely a stick attached to a rope but to the Mazeys it was an alibi.

THEY FOUND THE BODY, PARTIALLY COVERED BY WEEDS IN A DITCH IN THE OVERGROWN GARDEN

The boys had been playing. John had lost control and smashed straight into the tree, causing massive and fatal injuries. The brothers had panicked and hidden the body. They hadn't told their mother.

At the inquest on Saturday the Mazey story was quickly dismantled. Damning evidence was produced. Why had the Mazey boys gone round Kidwelly on Thursday trying to change a half sovereign? They had eventually changed it at Mrs. White's shop. They spent some of it but most of the change from that transaction was in their pockets when they were arrested. The rest they had hidden in a hedge. And why was it that when she was told about the body in her garden, Jane Mazey cried out "Oh my dear Benjamin! Poor little fellow!"?

The post mortem examination provided gruesome details that were unlikely to calm down an angry populace. The skull had been cracked open laterally across the forehead. The brain had disappeared, apart from a small portion that appeared to have been taken out and then replaced. The upper jaw was smashed, the lower jaw broken in 4 places. The body was almost completely drained of blood. There had been huge trauma to the head, caused it seemed by some sort of blunt instrument.

A new impression was now forming. That perhaps two young boys couldn't have inflicted such appalling injuries alone. It might have needed an adult. It might in fact have been Jane, the woman who told the frantically searching mother that it seemed as if the ground had swallowed him up. Perhaps the murder weapon was either the old spade or the mattock that were lying in the garden.

The family might have got away with the Fisher death. But not this time.

They were committed to trial in Swansea in May and were smuggled out of Kidwelly to Carmarthen gaol. To many there didn't seem to be much point. They'd done it. All they needed to find out was which one had hit him. Yet shockingly, in Swansea the family were found not guilty.

The boys blamed each other and tried their best to reduce their role in the tragedy. But there was a common thread to their stories. They had started to talk when they had been in transit to Carmarthen. Yes, John Thomas had been in the garden playing on the swing. According to Benjamin, John had climbed up on to a wall and suddenly fallen head first on to the flagstones. John managed to speak, "Oh Dai bach, rhoi dy law" ("David give me your hand") before he died. According to David, he had fallen through the roof of a derelict shed. After he hit the ground he said "Dai" three times and then expired.

They agreed that they carried the body to the top of the garden and tried to bury it. "Something white came out of the head. I took that and threw it across the road into Mrs. Gower's garden," said David. The brain. He then washed the blood away with water from a bucket. They agreed that they had taken the half sovereign.

They also agreed that they hadn't told their mother because they were afraid they would get beaten.

It was impossible to establish the precise details of what happened. The revelation that some of John's blood had been found on Jane's clothing merely added more uncertainty. Doctors confirmed that the injuries could have been caused by a fall but were not prepared to commit themselves. Today we can see the difficulties there might be in reaching a safe conviction.

The jury retired for only 5 minutes before returning their verdict of not guilty. The public however were less concerned with proof. They knew what had happened.

The Mazes had to leave Kidwelly. They didn't really have a choice. Innocent in the eyes of a few. Guilty in the eyes of the many. The town was set against them. The truth about what happened left Kidwelly with them. What they left behind them was a mystery and a tragedy.

And John of course. Beneath a fading stone in a distant cemetery. His life and his potential snuffed out so unexpectedly on that February afternoon, delivering shoes for his father. &

Based upon an article that first appeared in Welsh Country magazine in Sept/Oct 2006

Left: All Saints Church in Llansaint

Arthur Linton
DIED
1896
ABERDARE

You will find Aberdare Cemetery to the north of the town on the B4275. Head for Hirwaun along Cemetery Road to this very large cemetery.

From the main entrance, you must follow the bottom path that loops around towards the more modern section. Find Section C plot number E 6/16. Arthur is about 100 metres along on the left hand side. You are looking for a brown marble obelisk

It is extraordinary to think that a small place like the mining village of Aberaman, between Aberdare and Mountain Ash, should have produced four world class cyclists at the end of the nineteenth century.

There were the three Linton brothers - Arthur, Tom and Samuel - and their great rival Jimmy Michael. For a short time they were celebrities, particularly Arthur and Jimmy, both of whom became world champions.

It is Arthur though who is remembered in the very large Aberdare Cemetery, with his brown marble obelisk - and a spelling mistake, for on it he is called Lenton.

In memory of Arthur V. Lenton, son of John M. and Sarah Lenton of Aberaman who died July 23rd 1896 aged 28 years.

Also of the above John M. Lenton who died April 5th 1905 aged 62 years.

His was a sad and early death and a notorious one too, for Arthur Linton is regarded by some as the first victim of performance enhancing drugs in sport. The truth however is much less straightforward.

The end of the nineteenth century was an exciting time for cycling. The invention of the chain driven safety bicycle transformed the pastime. The old solid tyred penny farthing was awkward, uncomfortable and dangerous. Riding one was a rather dare-devil activity. But suddenly, with equal-sized wheels and pneumatic tyres, it became accessible to everyone. Suddenly cycling was all the rage. It became one of the great leisure pursuits, bringing an enormous boost to the market place. Races were soon organised by cycle manufacturers to promote their machines and to emphasise the speeds that could be achieved. Serious competitive races soon followed and before long there were professional riders employed by the manufacturers.

HIS WAS A NOTORIOUS DEATH, AS ARTHUR LINTON IS REGARDED BY SOME AS THE FIRST VICTIM OF PERFORMANCE ENHANCING DRUGS IN SPORT

THOSE WHO WISHED TO RACE HAD TO LOOK TO EUROPE AND SO IT WAS THAT, IN 1896, ARTHUR LINTON HAD HIS FINEST AND LAST VICTORY

The majority of professionals were working class boys, anxious to have the chance to race for the large cash prizes that were available. It was an attractive but dangerous cocktail; riders from poor homes prepared to take huge risks in the hope of transforming their finances, with manufacturers ready to take risks to increase market share. It isn't much different today. Cycling, along with boxing and football, is still seen on the Continent as a way in which talent, properly exploited, can liberate an individual and their family from a humble background. When the stakes are thus so high, who can condemn those who are prepared to bend the rules and take risks to help their family? These circumstances created a heady mix of intense competition and greed with young riders ready to push themselves to the limit and beyond. Soon it wasn't just speed that was important, it was endurance. Races became longer and longer and more demanding. The riders were routinely required to over-reach themselves.

Cycle clubs grew up everywhere. Aberdare Bicycle Club was formed and by 1890 had developed into a racing club.

Arthur Linton had started racing in the Cynon valley and his successes made him a well-known figure across South Wales. In 1893 he broke all the Welsh cycling records from five to twenty two miles. He was signed as a professional rider for the Gladiator Company. Here he worked under the trainer James "Choppy" Warburton from Lancashire. In 1894 Arthur broke four world records and defeated the French champion Dubois in Paris. He was declared Champion Cyclist of the World. On his return to Aberaman in December of that year he was received as a hero at a public banquet at the Lamb and Flag.

Another fact was that Choppy trained no less than three world champions during the 1890s. A great achievement but sadly he was, at best, a dodgy character. He was eventually banned from coaching because of rumours that his riders were being given large amounts of drugs. Suspicions were properly aroused when Jimmy Michael from Aberaman and another of his champions, collapsed with exhaustion in the middle of a track race. He remounted and set off once more. He did not notice that he was now cycling around the track in the opposite direction. Choppy may have trained winners, but he stored up huge problems that his riders carried with them into the future.

Road racing in England was increasingly difficult. Road traffic regulations were introduced that were designed to stop fast moving vehicles from frightening horses. This seriously inhibited road racing, which became a continental sport. So those who wished to race had to look to Europe and there it was in 1896 that Arthur Linton had his finest and last victory.

He was racing in the Bordeaux to Paris cycle race. It was an important race and the longest in the professional calendar. It covered 560 kilometres (350 miles) and was more than twice the distance of most single day races. It was known as the Derby of the road. Many of us would think that the race was unreasonably demanding. Many of us would think twice about doing this journey today in a car, without a reviving overnight stop. Plus of course Arthur was not only the

Rhondda Cynon Taf Libraries

THE MAJORITY OF PROFESSIONALS WERE WORKING CLASS BOYS, ANXIOUS TO HAVE THE CHANCE TO RACE FOR THE LARGE CASH PRIZES THAT WERE AVAILABLE

WHAT ARTHUR WAS GIVEN WAS PROBABLY HEROIN; OTHER DRUGS OF CHOICE WERE COCAINE AND STRYCHNINE

rider, but the mechanic too, carrying with him tools and spare tyres. He would have no one else to turn to. There was some back-up though, but of a very different kind.

In Arthur Linton's obituary in Cyclers' News the writer, who says he is 'one who knew him', reports:

> 'I saw him at Tours, halfway through the race, at midnight, where he came in with glassy eyes and tottering limbs and in a high state of nervous excitement. At Orleans at five o' clock in the morning, Choppy and I looked after a wreck - a corpse as Choppy called him, yet he had sufficient energy, heart, pluck, call it what you will, to enable him to gain 18 minutes on the last 45 miles of hilly road.'

We can't be sure what Choppy gave him, but it was almost certainly something a little stronger than encouragement. To recover 18 minutes of lost time in 45 miles, against competitors who themselves were striving their best to win, was remarkable. What he gave him was probably heroin.

The other drugs of choice were cocaine and strychnine, though none of them were really performance enhancing. All they did was to dull the pain and help the rider ignore the agony. Whatever it was, it enabled him to set a record time. So Arthur did win the race. But because he had taken a wrong turn somewhere along the route - not a surprise given the state he was in - he had to share the prize money with the second placed rider, Gaston Rivierre.

Arthur Linton died six weeks later in Aberdare in June 1896. He was 28 years old.

There are those who in these circumstances ascribe his death to the drugs he was given in his desperate attempt to win the prize money. Choppy Warburton was a notorious doper and obviously carried around with him a bulging bag of chemical tricks. Medication for every occasion. For him, sporting success was something that could be bought in a bottle. This would make Arthur Linton the first athlete to die from the modern curse of drugs within sport. Cycling as a sport, with its emphasis upon endurance and speed, is still ravaged by accusations of drug abuse. Thus Arthur was merely the first in a long list of distinguished names.

For some commentators therefore, Arthur has become famous by dying of strychnine or trimethyl poisoning. It was with Arthur that a curse began.

However, there are other opinions. There is no concrete evidence to link his death to his cycling. Contemporary reports say that he died of typhoid fever. This is possible too. Top level cycling can be especially unhealthy. The body is placed under tremendous strain in an unnatural position. Cyclists are always picking up infections, even today. The big races are constantly disrupted by riders withdrawing through viruses and stomach cramps. It is easy to take in unclean water offered by the side of the road when the riders are constantly trying to rehydrate themselves. Indeed, whilst Arthur's brother Samuel retired from cycling and returned to work in the collieries, his other brother Tom, who enjoyed a successful racing career, also died of typhoid fever in 1914.

If you want another interpretation then look at the report in The Herald Tribune. The editorial that reflected on the news of his death says that although the immediate cause of death was indeed typhoid:

> 'The collapse preceding his fatal illness was due to his riding extravagantly geared machines. The tendency to multiply gearing is too much prevalent. No constitution, however strong, can resist the terrible strain thrown upon the heart.'

Unnatural distances. Unnatural effort.

You can make your choice. Believe who you will. Arthur the hero of Aberdare was dead.

But what of the others in our story?

Choppy Warburton was found dead in a house in Wood Green in London in December 1897. All the money he possessed at the time of his death amounted to three half pennies.

Jimmy Michael retired from cycling and became a jockey and horse trainer in America. He died on an Atlantic liner in 1904 from an attack of 'delirium tremens' brought on by heavy drinking.

When Arthur Linton died the local community turned out to honour their sporting hero. His funeral was a huge affair and his cycle, draped in black crepe, was pushed behind the cortege. The tool of his trade and perhaps the instrument of his death, accompanying him to the grave. He was a young man from a poor community who died whilst seeking glory and wealth because he unexpectedly discovered that he had a talent that others were prepared to use. In this Arthur Linton of Aberaman is not unique. ✑

RESOURCES & ACKNOWLEDGEMENTS

A most important source for all these writings has been contemporary writings. In many cases, 'contemporary writings' has meant the Cambrian Newspaper. This was the first English language newspaper to be published in Wales, appearing between 1804 and 1930. It is an invaluable resource, full of national and local news and, like all newspapers, with a helpful interest in the shocking and the salacious.

There have been books too, which have been very helpful, and I am very grateful for the work that others have done which has often shown me the way.

Sian Busby's book about Sarah Jacob, called 'A Wonderful Little Girl' (published by Short Books in 2003) is a brilliant piece of work and essential reading for anyone who wants to find out more about this tragic case.

I am grateful for Peter Goodall's book, 'The Black Flag over Carmarthen' (published in 2005 by Gwasg Carreg Gwalch) where I first found out about Elizabeth Jones. Likewise the story of John Thomas first caught my attention in 'Kidwelly, Memories of Yesteryear' by Eric Hughes (published by the author in 2003). The quotations from the journal of Charlotte Johnes came from 'A Carmarthenshire Anthology' by Lynn Hughes (published in 1984 by Christopher Davies). The story of Mary Morgan is well-told in a little pamphlet called 'A Provincial Tragedy' written by Keith Parker, which you can obtain from the Judge's Lodging museum in Presteigne. Some information in the story of Arthur Linton was found in 'The Yellow Jersey, a Companion to the Tour de France' by Les Woodland (published by Ted Smart in 2003). Adrian Foster's guide to the history of Llanafan Fawr, which you can obtain from the Red Lion public house, was an invaluable resource for the story of John Price.

But of course, the most important thing of all has been the gravestones themselves.

Find them out.

Remember their stories.

Make sure that they are not forgotten.

Geoff

Geoff Brookes
Morriston, Swansea